THRIVE!

The Psychology Behind Achieving Professional Success

Jim Jawahar, PhD

Professor | Consultant | Editor

Editing, design, and distribution by Bublish

ISBN: 9781647046842 (eBook)
ISBN: 9781647046835 (paperback)
ISBN: 9781647046859 (audiobook)

Dedication

To Saira, Shawn, and Zach—

Thank you for your love and affection. Each of you have inspired me in unique ways, for which I am eternally grateful.

CONTENTS

ABOUT THIS BOOK

There are countless books on management, leadership, change, and other such topics pertaining to professional development and success. Most of these books are interesting and fun to read; some offer guidance on becoming successful based on anecdotal evidence, while others present thought-provoking insights into persistent problems, such as poverty or crime. However, very few of these books on management are based on research. Too often, after reading one of these books, if you were to ask yourself, "What did I learn, and how can I apply what I learned from this book to enhance my career?" you may not be able to list many takeaways. Even if you could, how would you know if those takeaways or suggestions will work for you? Just because a certain approach worked for one person does not mean it will work for you, because that advice was given based on anecdotal evidence, meaning it was not carefully tested or replicated in an unbiased, controlled environment. In contrast, suggestions based on the conclusions of careful experimentation and research are more likely to work. Thus, there is a need for books that elucidate concepts that have been rigorously tested and explain how these concepts can be successfully applied to achieve success. This book aims to fill this space.

In this book, eight individuals gather to spend a week at a lodge in the woods. The host, Professor James Mo, asks each of them to share their career journeys. After each individual shares their story, Professor James Mo explains the theoretical framework underlying their story—that is, the concepts and principles that contributed to the success of the individual. He then outlines the steps one could take to enhance their own success. Each story describes a pathway to success. This book then illustrates eight pathways to success, while acknowledging the existence of other pathways. Depending on your career circumstances, you could use one of these pathways or a combination of pathways to achieve your own success.

To be clear, success means different things to different people. For example, indicators of success might include reducing work stress, ensuring a fair workplace, enhancing workplace diversity, achieving psychological well-being, turning a boring job into an exciting and meaningful job, securing an excellent performance evaluation, obtaining a significant pay raise or a promotion, or moving up the corporate ladder. In addition, our definition of success will change as our careers evolve. For instance, a young professional might consider obtaining a promotion accompanied by a sizeable pay raise success, whereas a seasoned professional might consider managing to reduce work stress and achieving psychological well-being success.

To get the most value out of this book, read each of the eight career stories presented, study the theory Professor James Mo identifies as the root of that individual's success, and strategize ways to apply those principles to your own career. Then, engage in the exercises provided at the end of the book. Exercise 1 requires you to work individually, whereas exercise 2 requires a partner. These exercises involve clearly describing your current situation, outlining your aspirations, and identifying one or two pathways illustrated in the book that will best help you achieve your aspirations. Once you have identified the pathway(s), read that story again and write down how you might successfully apply the principles described in the pathway. Be sure to also outline a timeline, list the resources you may need, and anticipate the obstacles you may encounter. Refine your plan in the context of identified resources and constraints, implement your plan, and persist. I wish you much success!

INTRODUCTION

Professor James Mo—known as J Mo to his colleagues, students, and friends—walked across his university's campus to turn in his office keys. After spending nearly thirty-one years in academe, he had made the bittersweet decision to retire.

J Mo had an eclectic academic background with degrees in physics, industrial and organizational psychology, human resource management, and organizational behavior. As an intellectual, he thoroughly enjoyed philosophical thought and educated discussion. He was not a stereotypical professor—in fact, he was quite the opposite. He was clean-shaven, muscular, and looked more like an athlete than an academic. Like his father, J Mo never took a day off. He enjoyed working and considered his job to be fun. Most Saturday and Sunday mornings, he would be the only person working in his entire building. What others did or did not do mattered very little to him. His daily routine was to get up at 5:00 a.m., get ready, and go to work. He would be in his office before 7:00 a.m., work until 4:00 p.m., and then leave to go to the gym.

J Mo's work identity was wrapped around two things: being an educator and being a researcher. As an educator, he cared deeply about mentoring his students. He encouraged his students to critically examine ideas and concepts that contributed to their ability to achieve levels of success they never thought themselves capable of. Most students appreciated his passion for teaching. Some dreaded the amount of work in his classes. As a professor, he only taught two days a week, and he would always wear a suit and tie when teaching to convey the seriousness with which he approached this important work. His attire during nonteaching days was casual and usually included blue jeans or khaki pants and a black T-shirt or a black polo.

Even though J Mo spent eleven years as a university administrator, he viewed himself as a faculty member, and research was central to that identity. He truly enjoyed research and collaborating with groups of scholars on research projects. He particularly enjoyed working with junior scholars to teach them the craft of conducting high-quality research and developing the skills and ability to publish in reputed journals in the field.

After supper, J Mo would usually walk his dog, Zeus, a golden retriever. Sometimes, his wife, Dana, would accompany him on those walks. Late in the evening, while sipping a glass of whiskey, he'd catch up on his emails and do some light reading before going to bed.

J Mo was always busy, as it was his philosophy to work hard and to play hard. His sons played hockey for a travel team, which meant traveling to different cities to play in hockey tournaments. As an extroverted person, he really loved getting together with the hockey dads for drinks, and because of his love for Jameson, the hockey dads began calling him J Mo. The name stuck.

J Mo really enjoyed teaching and working with students on independent studies and research projects, but COVID-19 changed all of that. He, like most other faculty members, was forced to teach fully online. The spring semester of 2020 was brutal. J Mo had never taught an online course and had no knowledge of the university's learning management system before the pandemic. Thankfully, with the help of his colleagues and his youngest son, he quickly learned the basics of teaching a class online and how to use Zoom to conduct class.

Somehow, he survived that semester. Little did he know, however, that all classes would be fully online the following academic year.

■ ■ ■

Connecting with students in an online environment was a challenge. They weren't interested in his insights the way they used to be and simply wanted credit for attending the Zoom lecture and to leave as soon as it was over. As a result of these changes—in both environment and student enthusiasm—J Mo began to feel disconnected from his purpose and identity as an educator. He derived no joy from teaching online; it simply wasn't fulfilling. He knew his students did not like it either, and he felt badly for them. Indeed, they were being cheated out of the complete college experience.

J Mo had been contemplating retirement for a few years, even before the pandemic, and in the wake of his classes going digital, he began to consider it more seriously than ever. His retirement benefits were decent, he'd saved enough money, and he'd made some great investments early on. His wife, Dana, was bright and hardworking, and she had risen rapidly in the corporate hierarchy to achieve a senior executive position in a Fortune 500 company. She had retired a year prior and was loving it.

J Mo collaborated with several groups of colleagues from the US, Western Europe, and Asia on research projects, and he really enjoyed the intellectual stimulation. However, he was enjoying teaching less every year. The pandemic made his decision easier, and J Mo retired from university life, but not from research.

J Mo and Dana downsized from a five-bedroom house to a two-bedroom ranch house. Both he and his wife were nature enthusiasts and were contemplating buying a log cabin so they could have a place to get away.

Instead of buying just a log cabin, they ended up buying a lodge that had several cabins on its grounds. The lodge was three miles from a small rural town right on the Ohio River. It was in a wooded area with many trails and an abundance of lakes. The lodge owners had been losing money during the pandemic and could not pay the mortgage, so they were forced into foreclosure.

J Mo and his wife bought the entire lodge for just 30 percent of its pre-pandemic value, paying cash. The lodge had ten rooms, a huge master bedroom, a large entryway and sitting room, a full-sized commercial kitchen, and an outdoor firepit. It also came with a guesthouse located a hundred yards from the main lodge. Thankfully, Josh and his wife—tenants in the guest house—stayed on with J Mo. Josh took care of the grounds and all the maintenance work and Jean, his wife, prepared meals for the guests. She was a good cook, did the laundry, and took great care in keeping the lodge nice and clean. She would also help check in and check out guests. She took great pride in her work and took care of the place as if it were her own. Josh and Jean were only in their midfifties. Both were retired firefighters and enjoyed their semiretired lifestyle.

J Mo and Dana were in for an adventure, as neither of them had operated a business before. Although they liked the idea of being lodge owners, they were apprehensive of what the future held. Should they keep one cabin for themselves, try to rent out the other cabins, and have Jean take care of the day-to-day operations? They were not ready for the daily grind of managing the lodge; that wasn't part of their retirement plan.

The lodge required a face-lift, so after purchasing it, they replaced the dilapidated wooden floor in the entryway and the sitting room with new wooden floors, swapped most of the outdated furniture in the sitting room with modern-but-rustic furniture to make it nice and cozy, and installed brass fixtures and energy-efficient windows. Even factoring in the cost of repairs, they had purchased the lodge for less than 50 percent of its pre-pandemic appraised value. By the time the repairs and upgrades were finished, the lodge looked brand-new and inviting.

J Mo and Dana invited their friends to a grand opening—or *reopening*—of the lodge. After a sumptuous dinner, they gathered around the firepit, told stories, laughed, and danced. Everyone stayed overnight, and after a hearty breakfast the next day, they hiked one of the many trails nearby. Late in the afternoon, they went canoeing and did some fishing. As they gathered around the firepit that night, Michelle, one of Dana's closest friends, thanked them and said, "You should advertise an adventure package in a magazine like *Outside* and have guests stay for a week. You could take them hiking, canoeing, and fishing, and in the evenings, you could gather around the firepit and share stories."

Dana asked, "Do you think people would be interested enough in something like that to stay for an entire week?"

Megan and her husband, Stewart, said they would. Several others agreed, and J Mo's friend Peter said, "Stacy and I would love to do something like that. It would be great to get away from all the hustle and bustle of daily life and live for a week here in the open, carefree."

Dana and J Mo also liked the idea and after bouncing this idea off several friends, decided to give it a go. J Mo placed the following ad in the magazine *Outside*:

> Enjoy a weeklong Midwest adventure in the wilderness. Package includes your own cabin, gourmet meals, hiking, canoeing, and fishing. Enjoy late-night storytelling, dancing, or just chilling around an outdoor firepit. Visit JMoDanaLodge.com for details.

Within three days of the issue's publication, they received twelve inquiries, and after some back and forth, eight customers put down their deposits. This first set of guests would arrive in two weeks. J Mo and Dana decided they would have guests on alternate weeks, so they could rest up and recharge during the off weeks; this would also give J Mo time to read and continue his research pursuits.

Two weeks flew by, and on Sunday, the guests began to arrive, one by one. Three of the guests—Jill, Shawn, and Michael—had to be picked up at the airport. Josh drove to the airport to pick them up.

Dana and Jean had been working in the kitchen all afternoon, and dinner was served at 8:00 p.m. It was a balmy night with a slight breeze. After dinner, some of the guests, tired from their travels, retired for the night. Others hung around in the sitting area and were getting to know each other. The guests were informed that breakfast would be served at 8:00 a.m. the next morning and they would leave the lodge at 9:30 a.m. for a hike through the woods.

By 9:30 the next morning, John, Jill, Chris, Sarah, Shawn, Kim, Darnell, and Michael were all ready for their hiking trip. While they were visibly excited, it was also clear they were nervous. Four of them admitted they had never been hiking. Dana had prepared nine backpacks, each containing a boxed lunch, three bottles of water, some snacks, and a towel. J Mo led the way, and off they went. J Mo said they would hike three miles to one of the shallow lakes nearby, break for lunch and rest for an hour, then do some canoeing for a couple of hours before hiking back. The plan was to return to the lodge by five o'clock. Dinner would be served at seven, and after dinner, they would gather around the firepit for drinks and storytelling.

As they started to hike through the woods, it became clear several of the guests were out of shape. The group had to rest for a few minutes after every mile because they were tired of walking up and down steep slopes, and the twists and turns did not help either. They were glad to reach the lake and enjoy the boxed lunches Dana had prepared. John, Kim, and Sarah really enjoyed the canoeing experience—a first for them. Others had either canoed or kayaked before. By 3:30 p.m., it was time to hike back. Unbelievably, Darnell tried to call an Uber. Of course, there was no cell service, so they made the slow trek back to the lodge.

Dinner was trout, rice, roasted red potatoes, steamed carrots, and broccoli. Everyone cleaned their plates, and a few went back for seconds. By around eight o'clock, everyone—with a drink in hand—gathered around the firepit and started chitchatting. J Mo said, "There are eight of you, and the best way to really get to know each other is for you to tell us about yourself. I'm not talking about just saying a few sentences about yourself; I mean sharing your life story. I enjoy learning about people, and I'm especially interested in hearing about your careers, as I was once a professor who studied careers before retirement."

The group was silent. J Mo added, "Listen, you are perfect strangers, unlikely to see each other after this week, so there is little downside or risk to sharing your story." When somebody asked him if he was using their stories for his research, J Mo was slightly taken aback—that wasn't his original intention, but it seemed like a great opportunity to expand his knowledge on a subject that had largely been the focus of his career. "If I kept it anonymous, would you mind?" he asked the group, and nobody objected.

After that, the conversation took off, starting with John, who said, "I'm happy to go first."

Several in the group shouted, "You go, John!"

1

Forging High-Quality Relationships: Why Does Your Relationship with Your Supervisor Matter?

"I'm in a happy place now, career-wise," John began, "but that wasn't always the case. One day, a little over a year ago, I was driving home with a smile on my face because I felt the interview I'd just gone to had gone well. I was just grateful for the opportunity to interview for a job. I'd lost my six-figure job five months prior, and it turned my life upside down. I could not sleep well for days. I was restless, irritable, and depressed. I even made excuses when my friends asked why I didn't show up for bowling, my favorite activity. With every passing day, I was feeling less hopeful of finding a job that would pay as well as the one I had lost."

John leaned forward, resting his elbows on his knees. The firelight flickered over his features, and the forest around the group got quiet, as though it was listening in on the conversation just as raptly as everybody else. "You see, I went to a good school, I know my stuff, and I'm a hard worker. I always do a good job, and I'm generally well-liked by others. I have lots of friends and love to socialize. I can confidently say I didn't deserve to be fired. I wasn't the problem. The problem was my supervisor."

▓   ▓   ▓

J Mo cocked a brow, intrigued. His previous research had indicated job loss was often the result of interpersonal conflict—an interesting finding, considering that being fired should realistically be based on something more objective, such as work performance.

"I just couldn't see eye to eye with him," John went on, shaking his head. "Somehow my relationship with my supervisor had soured, and there was underlying tension between us. One day, my supervisor, a few colleagues, and I were discussing how best to meet the needs of a new client. This new client would account for 10 percent of the company's revenue if everything went well. As we discussed our ideas, there were debates. One thing led to another, and I ended up having a heated argument with my supervisor in front of my colleagues. The argument wasn't personal; it was simply a disagreement about how best to serve the client. I just couldn't believe my supervisor wouldn't accept my ideas, and I was frustrated—agitated, even—when he kept turning down my suggestions, one after the other. Sadly, this wasn't the first time we'd disagreed; it seemed like we were at odds more frequently in the last six months than in the past.

"The next day, I didn't feel like going to work. I seemed to have no energy, but I forced myself to get ready and drive to work. When I showed up, my supervisor called me into his office and told me I had crossed the line and I was fired. I was shocked; I couldn't believe it!

"I spent the next hour gathering personal effects and saying goodbye to colleagues, who were equally shocked and disgusted with my supervisor's decision. Walking out of the office building, I was angry, but I also felt a sense of shame and hopelessness. I felt bad for my family. I knew my wife would be devasted to hear I'd been fired.

"As I got into my car, I was thinking about how I would have to dip into our personal savings to pay the mortgage and other living expenses. Running the numbers in my head, I figured we could get by for a few months. The thought of having to deplete our savings made me angry and sad at the same time. I remember that day well. As I pulled into my driveway, I was greeted by my daughter, who was playing in the front yard, and by my wife when I entered the house.

"Anyway, back to the night I was driving home with a smile on my face—I had just finished an interview with the bank that I was feeling optimistic about. I wanted the job so badly, because my mental health had been deteriorating, and my wife and I seemed to be arguing more often than in the past. I was convinced going back to work would save me and our marriage.

"Five days after the interview, I received a call from Peter, the head of IT at the bank, who offered me the job. I was happy with the offer, as I would start as a network manager at a major bank. I was delighted to get my life back and looked forward to starting the new job in two weeks.

"That day, after dinner, I headed to my home office in our basement to call my close friends to share the good news. They were happy for me and wished me well. But, my closest friend, Mike, emphasized the importance of relationships at work. I immediately recalled my old job and felt bitter. To make ends meet, I'd had to pull Sally, our six-year-old, from her piano lessons, and she couldn't understand why, as I was the one who'd wanted her to learn to play in the first place.

"At that moment, I resolved to learn from my mistakes and began to jot down all the things I'd done right and all the things I'd done wrong at my previous job. As I was reviewing the list, it dawned on me that my biggest problem hadn't been that I'd confronted my supervisor in front of our fellow coworkers in an insubordinate way but that I had failed to forge a strong, healthy relationship with him from the start. Granted, he was an insecure, pompous, arrogant man, but in the end, it didn't matter—he was still my supervisor, and not having a good relationship with him cost me my job. I wrote down some ideas about how I would approach and relate with my new supervisor at the bank.

"Two weeks later, I started my new job. My coworkers threw a small reception at the end of the day to welcome me. During the reception, I had a pleasant conversation with my new supervisor, Peter. Peter mentioned he had to leave around 5:00 p.m. to go play in his bowling league. I was delighted Peter also belonged to a bowling league. We both chatted about how much we enjoyed bowling and exchanged notes about our respective leagues. I was glad to have something in common with him and that we had gotten off to a good start.

"Peter really enjoyed his work as the head of IT for the bank. He only wished he had more time to volunteer at his church and help his son's elementary school with their never-ending IT issues, such as slow network, storage issues, application malfunction, and a host of other problems. One day, as he got off the phone with the principal, who had called for advice, I walked into his office, as I needed Peter to sign off on some documents. Peter casually mentioned all the IT problems the school was experiencing. Without thinking, I told Peter, 'Our network systems are all fine; I can take off for a couple of hours this afternoon and swing by the school to diagnose the problems, if that's okay with you?' Peter was momentarily taken back, but after a few seconds, he smiled at my offer to help. After all, I was still a new employee and Peter didn't really know me that well.

"Peter seemed to realize the benefits of accepting my offer to help. If I could solve the problems, it would make him look good at the school, especially at school board meetings. Plus, he knew I was more technically capable and could get the job done in no time.

"Later that evening, after vising the school, I texted Peter, saying, 'Everything is resolved for now. Their server is very old and could give out any day, but I might have a solution. We can talk about it tomorrow.' The next morning, he came looking for me to thank me for helping with the school's IT issues. He also wanted to inquire about the solution. I mentioned the bank had two servers that were not being used and donating one to the school would not only benefit the school but would be a tax deduction for the bank. Peter liked the idea and said he would discuss it with the head of accounting and get back to me. A week later, I went to the school and installed the server donated by the bank, set up the network, and ensured all data were backed up. Done and done!

"Peter was excited when the principal called to thank him and commended me for doing such a great job of installing the server and resolving the IT issues, which the school had been facing for nearly two years. Peter seemed delighted and to show his appreciation, he offered to buy me drinks at the local bar after work. And it was Friday, so why not celebrate?

"At the bar, Peter and I talked about bowling. The conversation drifted to football, and I said I was the biggest Dallas Cowboys fan. Peter was surprised to hear that, as the Cowboys were also his favorite team. We talked about the good old days when Troy Aikman was the quarterback, Emmitt Smith was the running back, and Deion Sanders played as safety and wide receiver. Indeed, those were the glory days of the Cowboys.

"My wife, Diane, called to let me know her parents picked up Sally from school and that Sally will be spending the night with them. My wife said she was bored. I asked if she would like to join us at Mickey's, the bar close to the office, knowing how much she liked to party. Diane said she would be there in twenty minutes. I was thinking that after introducing Diane to Peter, we could split up and go to a nice restaurant for dinner. When Diane arrived, I introduced her to Peter, and she instantly recognized him. Apparently, they had both attended the same high school, and Peter, who'd played lacrosse, had been two years ahead of her in school. They spent the next hour talking about their high school days. Peter realized it was getting very late and he had to go home for dinner. As he was leaving, my wife said, 'Peter, you and your family should come over to our house for dinner some evening.' Peter said yes right away. After he left, Diane and I agreed it was a small world and headed out to dinner.

"My first month on the job, I spent a good deal of time studying the workflow in the network area, including what we were doing, why, and how. After several conversations with team members and internal clients, I was able to identify three things that could be done right away to improve efficiency and two other things that could be done over the next three to six months. I put together an improvement plan and discussed it with Peter. Peter was impressed with my insights and ideas and immediately asked me to go ahead with implementing those solutions. Two weeks later, I asked Peter if he had received any feedback about the improvements made. Peter indicated even the higher-ups had noticed the positive improvements and thanked me for being proactive. I asked him to let me know if there were any other improvements I could make.

"I really liked working at the bank. I'm a pretty laid-back guy who likes to help others, and I have a lot of positive energy that sometimes seems to rub off on others. Once a week, I'd take my team members to lunch so I could get to know them better. I wanted a create a positive work environment.

"One afternoon, we were busy preparing for the quarterly meeting with the Feds that was coming up. In case you didn't know, the Feds meet with bank officials on a quarterly basis to ensure compliance and monitor risk mitigation efforts. I was busy getting ready and noticed Peter was apprehensive about the meeting. At the last meeting, the bank had been cited on several issues related to IT, so there was good reason for Peter's apprehensiveness. One of the issues pertained to data security. The head of information security, Frank, was very competent technically but was not a very good communicator. In fact, his team did not like working for him; allegedly, he did not always give them clear instructions or thank them for their work.

"Thankfully, I was able to easily respond to the questions from the Feds pertaining to my area of responsibility. But Frank's presentation prompted more questions, and the Feds had difficulty understanding his explanations. The Feds made him nervous, and he knew his communication skills weren't very good. When he got nervous, he spoke fast, and when he spoke fast, his accent made it difficult for others to understand him. He was fine in one-on-one conversations, but groups made him uncomfortable. Because of my familiarity with security issues from my previous job, I elaborated on some of Frank's responses, and the Feds seemed satisfied. Peter was relieved and later told me I had saved the day.

⬛   ⬛   ⬛

"A few weeks later, Frank announced his resignation, as he wanted to move to Atlanta to be closer to his brothers. He was going to head security at a global food services company, and he was happy about the new job, as he did not have to deal with the Feds anymore.

"The sudden departure of Frank created a managerial void, and Peter acknowledged it was not going to be easy to hire for the position on such short notice. At the same time, he needed someone to head security, and unfortunately employees in that area were not very experienced and did not have the leadership abilities to head IT security for the bank.

"Naturally, I offered to help. I told Peter I was familiar with the security operation and could lead that area until someone else was hired. Peter agreed and thanked me for stepping up.

"On the day we hosted Peter's family for dinner, my wife had been cooking and cleaning all day. It was nearly 5:00 p.m., and the guests would be arriving at around six. Sally was excited to meet seven-year-old Caden. When our guests arrived, Peter introduced his wife, Megan, to me and went straight to the kitchen to find Diane to pick up their conversation about their high school days. Caden and Sally went to the backyard to play. The adults settled in the kitchen. My wife and Megan got along well, and Megan relished hearing stories about Peter from his high school days.

"Six months after I'd started working at the bank, Peter called me into his office and gave me my first performance review. The review was extremely positive, and the feedback glowing. In fact, I have never received such high praise! I felt good about myself. Finally, things were going my way. I felt appreciated, empowered, and important, and it felt good to feel that way. I went back to my office and called my wife right away to share the news. She was very happy for me. Life was good.

"The next meeting with the Feds was right around the corner, and Peter and I were busy getting ready for it. I did a good job of covering the network area and conveying all the progress made during the last quarter, with reference to the citations received pertaining to security issues. The Feds were satisfied with my updates regarding what had been done and with my plans for the future. I felt Peter respected me and trusted me to not only do my job well but also find ways to make things better. I had proven myself and demonstrated my loyalty. I made Peter look good, which was very important to him, as he aspired to, one day, become the chief operating officer.

"Two weeks later, the entire security team requested to meet with Peter. Peter did not know what to make of it. Apparently, during the meeting, the team informed him I was a good leader, I communicated my appreciation of them regularly, and I also inspired them to higher levels of productivity. They reported I made work fun. In fact, they wanted me to be their permanent boss. Peter was delighted to hear such positive comments, even though he already knew I was doing a good job of keeping things working smoothly.

"Peter, after consulting with the chief operating officer, promoted me to the role of director of network and data security. The promotion came with a $30,000 bump in pay. I was ecstatic! With such a huge raise, I could finally take my family for a nice vacation that summer—something I couldn't do the summer before when I did not have a job. Sally would be thrilled; she had always wanted to go to the beach."

John's energy was tangible, prompting everybody in the group to smile. He sat back in his chair, sighing with relief. "Recently—just three weeks ago, in fact—I attended the Annual Security Conference. I was invited to sit on a panel and had an opportunity to discuss what our bank was doing to secure its data and applications. After becoming director, I had implemented several new measures to improve security and safeguards against cyberattacks. Although nothing is foolproof, many in the audience appreciated my knowledge and willingness to share best practices and insights. Peter was in the audience and later told me my presentation and discussion brought additional recognition to the bank. I am grateful to Peter for giving me the opportunity to showcase my talents. We not only like each other and trust each other but we also have mutual admiration for each other. It has been an exciting, jam-packed year—but an excellent one! I needed a break, and here I am."

Everyone thanked John for sharing his story. Kim commented about the detail and thoroughness of the story and said, "Well done, my friend. You set the bar pretty high."

After a bit of laughter from the group, J Mo took a sip of his drink and asked, "John, what do you think was the root of your success in your new position with the bank? What do you think contributed most to your promotion and raise?"

John replied, "The root of my success is that I have a great supervisor."

J Mo chuckled, shaking his head. "No, you were successful because you were able to forge a high-quality relationship with your supervisor. That is why." He turned to face the others in the group. "Let me tell you about the theory behind strong, high-quality relationships, how these relationships develop, and the benefits of such relationships."

UNDERLYING THEORETICAL FRAMEWORK

There are many leadership theories, and leader-member exchange (LMX) theory is one of them. LMX theory is a popular approach to explain the quality of relationships between a leader and his followers.

As you know, leaders don't treat all their team members the same way. They often differentiate among team members and develop either high- or low-quality relationships with team members. The quality of the exchange relationship has consequences for both the leader and the follower. Research has identified several antecedents and consequences of the quality of the leader-member exchange relationship.

How Do These Relationships Develop and What Are the Consequences?

Like in any other friendship, team members who have things in common with their manager have a better chance of developing a good relationship with their manager. Employees who go above and beyond in cooperating with their manager's leadership—as well as having the willingness and enthusiasm to resolve organizational issues independently, without being prompted—are incredibly likely to forge a healthy relationship with their supervisor. This relationship should, of course, not only be one of mutual benefit but one that contributes to the overall success of the company.

Managers depend on cooperative subordinates and are likely to reward their cooperation with a variety of benefits and opportunities, such as trusting them to handle challenging assignments, offering mentorship, granting access to information, giving positive performance evaluations, and offering promotions. High-quality relationships are based on mutual obligation and reciprocity, characterized by mutual liking and respect, and are often transformational in nature.

In contrast, employees who do not strive to discover common ground with their managers, who do not socialize or show initiative in their role in the company, and who are only willing to do the bare minimum are less likely to establish a positive relationship with their supervisors. Such relationships are often formal, contractual, quid pro quo exchanges and usually feel transactional in nature. Subordinates in low-quality relationships with their managers typically receive lower performance evaluations and are often passed over when it comes to promotional opportunities.

John failed to establish a high-quality relationship with his first manager because they had very little in common and had a conflicting power dynamic. However, he learned from that experience and succeeded in forging a high-quality relationship with his second manager, Peter. How did this come about?

First, he had two things in common with Peter: bowling and football. In fact, they both had the same favorite NFL team—the Cowboys. Finding common ground suggests you have similar interests or viewpoints, giving a context for the conversation to occur.

Second, they socialized outside of work—spending time in a bar over drinks, and later, the families got together for dinner at John's residence. Socializing in a relaxed, informal environment outside of work further cemented their liking for each other.

Third, John went to Peter with ideas to improve the work done in his area, implemented his ideas effectively, and sought further feedback. Suggesting ways to improve work procedures and processes shows initiative, is proactive in nature, and is often appreciated.

Fourth, John enhanced the work environment with his positive attitude and cheerful personality, making it a fun place to work. He galvanized his team by taking them out to lunch and expressing a genuine interest in their personal and professional happiness.

Fifth, John volunteered to help resolve the school's IT issues and came up with a creative solution to the problem. In doing so, he made Peter look good, which was important for Peter's ego. John went out of his way to do a favor for Peter, and the social exchange principle—the idea that favors accepted must be repaid in kind at some point so that the exchange of favors can continue—suggests the favor will be returned in kind.

Sixth, John was competent in his position, which was evident during his first meeting with the Feds.

Seventh, John helped answer some of the questions meant for Frank, demonstrating he was a team player.

Eighth, at a critical juncture, John stepped up to fill the void left by Frank's departure.

Because of the high-quality relationship John established with Peter, he was permitted to take on the challenging assignment of filling in for Frank when he quit, which was another opportunity for him to prove himself in his role within the company. This compounded his high-quality relationship with Peter, yielding high performance evaluations and his promotion to the role of director of network and data security with a substantial pay raise.

HOW TO APPLY THESE IDEAS TO ACHIEVE SUCCESS

Jill's brows furrowed. "What if you have nothing in common with your supervisor? What then?"

"You can always find something in common if you look hard enough," J Mo said. "Try to tactfully gather as much information as you can about your supervisor from your coworkers, especially from those already close with them. Your supervisor might have a favorite sports team, or they might be a foodie or a wine connoisseur. They may enjoy reading a certain genre of books, love to exercise, and so on. If your supervisor is passionate about something, develop an interest in that area—or at least some knowledge on the subject—so you will have something in common. Having things in common gives you a context to carry on a conversation.

"If you have very little in common, develop a high level of expertise in at least one area, so your supervisor comes to rely on you for that expertise. This is another way to lay the groundwork for developing a high-quality relationship. Of course, you still need to perform at a high level, volunteer, show you are a team player, maintain a positive attitude, and do things to make your supervisor look good."

IN WHAT SITUATIONS WILL IMPLEMENTING THESE IDEAS BE MOST EFFECTIVE?

The best time to implement these strategies is during the process of transitioning to a new job or upon the arrival of a new supervisor. Each of these scenarios provide a fresh start to establish a high-quality relationship with your supervisor, which will positively contribute to your career. Having a high-quality relationship will also enhance mental well-being, as it ensures your supervisor will not take advantage of you. In fact, he or she will look after you and care for your well-being.

WHAT IF YOU ARE ALREADY IN AN ESTABLISHED RELATIONSHIP WITH YOUR SUPERVISOR AND IT ISN'T GOING WELL?

Repairing a relationship is hard work. What most often holds us back is our ego. Let go of your ego and ask for a meeting with your supervisor. Ask for advice on how to become a valuable member of the team. Be sure to follow up frequently with your supervisor on how you are working on their advice. Over time, this will help change their perception of you, and you may be able to forge a better relationship with them as a result. In addition, you need to do all the things mentioned earlier, such as excelling at your job, becoming a team player, volunteering, showing initiative, and engaging in activities that make your team and your supervisor look good.

J Mo turned away from Jill, acknowledging John now. "Thank you, John, for telling such a great story. We all learned something today. It is getting late. Remember, breakfast is at 8:00 a.m., and we leave at 9:30. I'm going to call it a day. Don't stay up too late."

Everyone echoed J Mo's thanks to John, and then they thanked J Mo for his elaboration on the strategy behind John's success with his supervisor, Peter.

2

Go Big or Go Home vs. Small Wins and Self-Efficacy

The following day began with hiking to a nearby lake, where the group would go fishing. J Mo had reserved a boat that included all of the fishing gear they would need. Several attendees had never been fishing before, so J Mo and Josh ran around tagging baits and untangling fishing lines.

Later, Jill caught what must have been one of the biggest trout in the lake. Darnell gave up fishing and started reading a book. Between the ten of them, they caught twenty-eight fish and released six back, as they were too small. Jokingly, J Mo said, "We will be having trout again for dinner tonight!" Then he added, "Actually, Dana and Jean are preparing juicy steaks for dinner."

After dinner, the group gathered around the firepit as they had the night before.

J Mo sat back in his seat, regarding the people encircling the firepit, and said, "Okay, who wants to share their story next?"

There was silence until Jill bravely volunteered.

Jill took a generous sip of her wine before saying, "I started with G&C as an HR generalist about six years ago. I established myself as a solid contributor and was well-liked, so when the director of human resources left, I got his job. I had the credentials and support of upper management. I really enjoyed the job, my colleagues, the fast-paced nature of the industry, and working with smart people. You may not know this, but G&C is a midsized company in Silicon Valley and is a leader in managing clinical trials for major drug companies. The work itself was exciting and attracted top talent to the company.

"My husband—now ex-husband—and I were college sweethearts. We'd been together for fifteen years and married for twelve. We got married as soon as we found out I was pregnant. We are both ambitious professionals and devoted a lot of time to our jobs, which strained the relationship. Over the last five years of our marriage, we were drifting apart and seemed to have less and less in common, which was unfortunate. Finally, we divorced last year, as the chemistry between us had completely dissipated. We are on good terms. Joe works for a venture capital firm and makes a lot of money, so he offered me a generous settlement in return for joint custody of our eleven-year-old daughter, Melody.

"Last May, I obtained an MBA from San Jose State University, and to fully leverage my educational attainment, I felt it was the right time to move to another company. However, I liked my job and my colleagues, and I was paid well, so I wasn't in any hurry. I decided to be selective in my job search. The vice president of HR job at Innorex, Inc.—a pharmaceutical company—seemed like a great fit, as I knew a great deal about clinical trials. It would also mean I could continue living in the same house. It seemed like the perfect opportunity.

"So, I applied for the job and attended three interviews. I was a finalist for the position and was cautiously optimistic. A few days later, I was offered the position. I was able to negotiate a good package and was happy to start the new job in a month. Saying goodbye to my coworkers at G&C was bittersweet, and I had to fight back tears.

"Innorex, Inc. has 8,500 employees, which is much larger than the 1,200 employees at G&C. This meant I went from supervising two employees to supervising four managers—directors for talent management, compensation/benefits, employee relations, and human resource information systems. Each of these directors has five to eight direct reports. These direct reports are all managers who each supervise four to nine employees. My work was cut out for me, as I was transitioning from managing a team of HR professionals to managing a large HR organization.

"I spent the first month talking to the directors, managers, and employees to better understand the company's human resource policies and procedures. I also met with my peers to familiarize myself with their expectations and explored ways in which HR could behave like a true business partner. I collected a lot of information, which took me a couple of weeks to process. Soon, I realized two of my areas—talent management and compensation/benefits—were not effective. In fact, the two areas were dysfunctional and had outdated policies and procedures.

"Talent management includes recruitment and selection, onboarding, training and development, and succession planning. Major activities in the compensation/benefits area include maintaining up-to-date job descriptions, performing job evaluations, reviewing market surveys, adjusting pay structure, documenting performance evaluations, and ensuring pay raises stay within budget.

"I debated initiating large-scale changes, as completely overhauling both of these areas seemed warranted. However, since nothing seemed broken and no one was complaining, I decided against such a strategy. Instead, I focused on making small changes, because I was afraid of making a big change and failing.

"I decided to first focus on one area: recruitment. I reviewed workplace demographics and was shocked to find a lack of diversity at Innorex. This was perplexing to me, as Silicon Valley itself has a high level of diversity, with nearly 35 percent of those working in the area self-identifying as Asian and 25 percent as Hispanic and Latino.

"I needed to know more, so I asked for a table summarizing data from the last five years. It was to be organized by job title and show diversity rate—by race and sex—of both the applicant pool and of hires. Two things stood out. First, as expected, diversity among hires was low. Second, diversity rates in the applicant pool were also low. How could this be, given the location of Innorex in the heart of Silicon Valley?" Jill paused to look at everybody in the circle, her eyes landing eventually on J Mo, who listened intently. "Obviously, the company wasn't using the sources and methods necessary to reach a diverse applicant pool. So, I decided to focus on just one job—the business analyst position, as it was the job with the highest volume of new hires. This was an almost entry-level position requiring just one to two years of previous work experience in a similar position or solid internship or co-op experiences. With the help of my assistant, I made a list of magazines that target Asians and Hispanics, associations these groups belong to, as well as Hispanic-serving churches and Hindu temples. I ensured every position opening would be posted at these places in addition to the company's website and major job boards.

"Second, I contracted with an outside firm to create a training video for search committees, and with the help of the CEO, developed a policy that made it mandatory for every hiring manager and the hiring team to undergo search committee training prior to posting a job ad.

"Third, I hired outside consultants to work with managers in areas with a high volume of hiring. These consultants updated the existing job description of the business analyst position and developed a structured interview. Working with managers, these consultants identified tasks important to the job, then identified important knowledge, skills, and abilities required to perform those tasks. They then developed a set of questions to assess the knowledge, skills, and abilities they had previously identified. They went so far as to also develop a scale to rate responses to those questions, making sure the anchors used to score responses were specific and unambiguous, with clear examples of what constituted an excellent, average, or poor response.

"I convinced my peers that diversity was not an HR issue—it was *everyone's* issue. I told them that unless line managers took it seriously, diversity wasn't going to improve. And in order for line managers to take it seriously, it must be championed by upper management.

"Over time, we realized our efforts were paying off. Tracking indicated both diversity of applicant pools and diversity of hires were increasing. I was excited with the progress made and had demonstrated that diversity—in this one position, at least—could be enhanced. These data were enough to convince the CEO to expand this approach to other jobs for which the company hired new employees in large numbers on a regular basis. Slowly but surely, I was increasing diversity in the pipeline.

"After that, I turned my attention to the second area of concern: compensation. Along with the Director of compensation and the manager responsible for overseeing the pay structure, I reviewed the data. Examining the data by job title, I noticed a wide variation in salary. I focused my attention on the job that had the most employees, and the pattern was similar. To drill down even deeper, I put together a small team of analysts whose job it was to code the information of all employees in the job as follows: employee ID number, highest level of education attained, years since bachelor's degree obtainment, years of work experience, years in current job, race, sex, two most recent annual performance evaluations, and salary. This project took a week to complete, as there were 450 employees in this job.

"I used a statistical software called SPSS—Statistical Package for the Social Sciences—and used a technique called 'multiple regression' to analyze the data. In this technique, there are multiple independent variables and one dependent variable. In this case, the dependent variable was salary. The objective was to see which of these independent variables explained variation in the dependent variable—salary. As you can guess, performance evaluations and years of work experience explained significant variation in salary, which makes sense. People who have more work experience make more money, and people who are performing better make more money. But there were some surprising results, too. Sex was negatively related, meaning women were making less money than men, even after controlling for other independent variables in the multiple regression. Although race was also related to salary, given the small number of Asians, Hispanics, and African Americans in the company, the regression estimates for these individual groups were unlikely to be stable, so we couldn't be confident in the results. So, I recoded race as majority and minority—combining all non-whites into the minority category—and reran the multiple regression. Sure enough, whites made more money than non-whites.

"These results could mean one of two things, or perhaps both. The first was the possibility the white and male demographic received higher pay raises, which over time could explain the salary difference. The second possibility could have pertained to the starting salaries of these groups. Suppose women and minorities were hired at lower salaries, then over time, even if they received the same percentage of pay raises, there would still be a difference in salary. Or, again, it could be both that women and non-whites have lower starting salaries *and* the gap widens each year because they received lower pay raises than men and whites.

"I shared this information with the chief operating officer, an older and social justice–minded individual. He could not believe it and was visibly upset with these initial results. He wanted to get to the bottom of it and encouraged me to continue my research. Sure enough, data indicated that, all things being equal, women and non-whites were offered lower starting salaries relative to men and whites. They also received a lower percentage of pay raises, indicating both factors contributed to the salary differential. Was the difference in salary an outcome of intentional systemic racism or unconscious bias? Regardless, the big question was how to fix it, of course, without blaming anyone.

"One option was to completely overhaul the pay structure and the compensation function. That would be a major, monumental change to accomplish—one which I concluded would most likely fail, considering the turmoil it would cause. Also, it might have jeopardized my job. After all, the majority benefit from the status quo and would be against any large-scale change. The CEO and the board may have had to get involved, taking time and attention away from regular business issues. I was savvy enough to realize I was still new to the company and did not have much political capital to spend.

"After a great deal of thinking, I realized it would be easier to address the starting salary issue than the pay raise issue. A policy requiring HR authorization before making an offer was likely to help curb or even eliminate the practice of offering different starting salaries based on race and sex.

"The second issue, performance appraisals and pay raises, was a complicated one. Pay raises were based on performance evaluations, and men and whites received higher pay raises because of higher performance appraisal ratings. I realized there were a lot of factors that could explain differences in performance ratings, such as volunteering, showing initiative, or working on special projects. If supervisors intentionally or unintentionally offered extra resources to men and whites, then they might contribute more, deserve higher performance evaluations, and therefore be entitled to higher pay raises compared to women and minorities. Given the difficulty in verifying the accuracy of performance evaluations, I realized the practical difficulties associated with addressing this issue. You can't simply require supervisors to give women and minorities the same performance ratings as given to men and whites to ensure all groups receive the same percentage of pay raises.

"In the end, I ended up working with the COO to develop a policy that required line managers to receive HR authorization before making a salary offer to new hires. HR would compare the salary offer to salaries of other employees for a given job and look for any disparities based on race and sex before authorization. Any counter offers had to be approved by HR as well.

"Before rolling out the new policy, I met with my fellow vice presidents to discuss everything—the rationale for the policy and how the policy should be communicated with hiring managers specifically. All the vice presidents were on board. I made sure the process for reviewing and approving salary offers was streamlined and only took twenty-four hours or less. For the last 125 offers made, there was virtually no difference between starting salaries of new employees based on race or sex. I realized tackling the discrepancy in performance ratings and pay raises would have to wait another day and did not have the appetite to tackle it right away.

"Diversity is an important issue. It is a business imperative, and I care about it deeply, so I'm glad we are making progress as a company. Hopefully, slowly but surely, we will get there. So that is my story. With the divorce, starting a new job, and the day-to-day stress, I need a getaway, time to reflect, refresh, and rejuvenate. And here I am, sharing my life story with strangers but soon to be best friends," she said with a smile, and everyone laughed.

"Jill," said Sarah, "you are a smart cookie."

"I don't know about that," Jill said with a bit of a blush. "I had my doubts when I was making small changes instead of big ones, but luckily things turned out well."

J Mo chimed in. "Jill, it wasn't luck that contributed to your success. It was the science behind the strategy."

"What strategy are you talking about?" Michael asked. "Please give us your professional insights."

UNDERLYING THEORETICAL FRAMEWORK

"There is a famous social psychologist named Karl Weick who is a professor emeritus at the Ross School of Business at the University of Michigan," J Mo began. "Professor Weick introduced the concept of what he called 'small wins'—a strategy wherein a series of concrete, complete outcomes of moderate importance build a pattern that attracts allies and deters opponents. The concept of small wins incorporates sound psychological principles and is a pragmatic approach to bring about change.

What Happens When a Small Win Is Accomplished?

"Once a small win is accomplished, forces are set in motion that favor another small win. When a solution is put in place, the next solvable problem often becomes more visible. This occurs because new allies bring new solutions with them, and additional resources also flow toward winners, which means slightly larger wins can be attempted."

John asked, "Can you give us some examples that are based on the concept of small wins?"

"A well-known group that routinely uses this principle is Alcoholics Anonymous. Alcoholics Anonymous has been successful in helping alcoholics at least in part because it does not focus on abstaining from alcohol for the rest of one's life. While that is the goal of the program, alcoholics are told to stay sober one day at a time—or even one hour at a time, if temptation is high. Thus, the impossibility of lifetime abstinence is scaled down to the more workable task of not taking a drink for the next twenty-four hours, drastically reducing the size of a win necessary to maintain sobriety."

"Why do small wins work?" Jill asked.

"Small changes are preferred to large changes," John explained. "The small scale of small wins is important affectively as well as cognitively. Examples are plentiful. Successive small requests are more likely to produce compliance.

■　　■　　■

"Social comparison is more stable when the comparison leads to bonding over similarities rather than conflicting over differences. Small discrepancies, from an adaptation level, are interpreted as more pleasurable than larger discrepancies. Extremely easy or extremely difficult goals are less compelling than goals that feel immediately gratifying and easier to achieve. Learning tends to occur in small increments rather than in an all-or-none fashion.

"The point is that incremental phenomena, such as small wins, have a basic compatibility with human preferences for learning, perception, and motivation. Small wins are not only easier to comprehend but more pleasurable to experience.

"While no one denies winning big is a thrill, big wins can also be disorienting and can lead to unexpected negative consequences. Big wins evoke big countermeasures and alter expectations, both of which make it more difficult to gain the next win. For instance, the attention paid to Nobel Prize winners often makes it impossible for them to do any further significant work.

"When a large problem is broken down into a series of small wins, three things happen. First, the importance of any single win is reduced, in the sense that the costs of failure are small and the rewards of success considerable. Second, the size of the demand itself is reduced. And third, the effort feels feasible to accomplish with one's existing set of skills. A small win reduces importance, reduces demands, and raises perceived skill levels. So the mindset is, *This is no big deal, that's all that needs to be done*, and *I can do at least that*."

J Mo continued, "Jill used this idea of small wins to succeed. When she concluded two of her areas were dysfunctional, she did not immediately plan to make wholesale changes. Although such changes may have been warranted, the risk of failure was greater. She focused on one small problem at a time. While diversity was lacking in the entire company, which was a *big problem*, she chose to focus on increasing diversity of the applicant pool in just one job, which was a *smaller problem*."

"I see what you're saying." Jill's brows furrowed with thought. "By focusing on the small problem that could be solved in a reasonable amount of time, I was able to take the first step in solving the bigger, overarching problem that demanded a lot more time, skill, and effort."

"Exactly," J Mo replied with a smile. "Likewise, salary differences existed across the company. Instead of suggesting wholesale changes in the compensation system of the company, which also had a higher risk of failure, Jill chose to focus on salary differences in just one job and performed an in-depth analysis. She decided trying to solve the problem entirely through a multipronged approach would be too overwhelming and would likely be met with resistance. So, she did the smart thing. She developed a strategy she could control by creating a policy requiring HR's approval of salary figures.

"Utilizing the concept of small wins to bring about change has another important benefit: it enhances your self-efficacy. Albert Bandura, a professor at Stanford University, introduced the concept of self-efficacy in the late 1970s. Self-efficacy is defined as the belief in one's capabilities to mobilize the motivation, cognitive resources, and courses of action needed to meet given situational demands. Since its introduction, self-efficacy has emerged as one of the most frequently studied constructs in psychology and organizational behavior, primarily because it has been found to predict several important work-related outcomes, including job attitudes, training proficiency, and job performance. In addition, self-efficacy is seen as a personal resource with potential to buffer the stressor-strain relationship. According to Bandura, sources of self-efficacy beliefs include mastery or direct experience, vicarious experience, verbal persuasion, and affective arousal." J Mo paused to consider his audience's reaction, allowing the information he'd just delivered to sink in. "I bring this up because directly experiencing a small win is the most powerful booster of self-efficacy. In Jill's case, her initial success boosted her self-efficacy beliefs, positioning her well for the next small win. When you are a winner, you attract allies and deter opponents, which further increases your chances of success. Jill attracted allies in the form of fellow vice presidents and the COO, which further increased her chances of achieving success."

THE FALLACY OF "GO BIG OR GO HOME"

"Now," J Mo went on, swirling the whiskey in his hands, "this leads us to discussing the fallacy of what most people call 'go big or go home'— or essentially a do-or-die mentality regarding what they are trying to accomplish."

Wouldn't that fire-under-your-butt approach work, though?" Jill asked, and several of the others nodded in agreement.

"The massive scale on which social problems are conceived often precludes innovative action, because conceiving problems on a massive scale taxes the limits of bounded rationality and raises our arousal to dysfunctionally high levels," J Mo replied. "People often define social problems in ways that overwhelm their ability to do anything about them, right?"

"I suppose that makes sense," Darnell said. "Could we get an example?"

J Mo gave him a nod, eyes twinkling. "To understand this phenomenon, consider the following descriptions of the problems of hunger, crime, and traffic congestion. To reduce domestic hunger, we grow more food, which requires greater use of energy for farm equipment, fertilizers, and transportation, all adding to the price of energy, which then raises the cost of food, putting it out of the price range of the needy. To solve the problem of soaring crime rates, cities expand the police force, which draws funds away from other services such as schools, welfare, and job training, and thus inevitably leads to more poverty, addiction, prostitution, and more crime. To ease traffic congestion, multilane highways are built, drawing people away from mass transit, meaning the new road soon becomes as overcrowded as the old road. When social problems are described this way, efforts to convey their gravity disable the very resources of thought and action necessary to change them. When the magnitude of a problem is scaled upward in the interest of mobilizing action, the quality of thought and action declines, because processes such as frustration, arousal, and helplessness are activated.

"Big solutions, then, seem to elicit resistance, sabotage, and a host of dysfunctional behaviors. Now, this is not to say that systems and processes in companies don't need to be overhauled from time to time. The point is to start small, get a win, get the next win, and so on—chipping away at the problem slowly rather than tackling it all at once."

How to Apply These Ideas to Achieve Success

The fire had begun to grow low, burning to a heap of smoldering coals. Dana disappeared for a few moments, returning with a few logs to toss onto the fire. It was getting late, but it was clear the conversation was flowing and people wanted to stay out a little later than usual to hear the rest of J Mo's teachings.

With the fire stoked back to life, J Mo continued. "To successfully bring about change, recast big problems into small problems." He gestured to Jill. "Diversity in the workforce versus diversity in this one specific position, for example. Make sure you find a concrete solution to the problem. Solving the problem results in a small win and winning attracts allies and deters opponents. More importantly, it boosts self-efficacy, or one's confidence in tackling the next problem. Pretty soon, you are on your way to bringing about positive change."

In What Situations Will Implementing
These Ideas Be Most Effective?

"Calling for wholesale change will almost always be met with resistance, and initiating such a change will most likely fail, because those who are benefitting from the status quo will obviously object to a paradigm shift that would jeopardize their personal benefit. For this reason, it's obviously a better strategy to focus on small wins over a full-blown overhaul, as those small wins will build up and achieve the overall goal—but they will do so in a way that will likely fly under the radar of the people most motivated to stand in the way of it. An example of this is local change that eventually builds to global change.

"Now, let's get back to applying this strategy on a corporate level. If you are new to the company or to the job, you may not have, as Jill called it, enough *political capital* accumulated to spend to bring about a big change. In such cases, it is best to use the small wins strategy. Once a small win is achieved, you will attract allies, and with their support, you can attempt the next small win.

"This is not to say that aspirational goals or bold vision statements are unimportant—in fact, quite the contrary. If you are a CEO or a senior executive, you should establish compelling vision statements and aspirational goals for the company or for your area, such as HR, for example. Again, if nothing is broken, or if you feel you don't have the political capital, you could still use the small wins strategy to work toward those aspirational goals."

J Mo gestured to Jill, who was sitting across the fire from him. "Although Jill wasn't familiar with the concept of small wins, she inadvertently used the right strategy to tackle the problem, and that was why she was successful in her effort to effect change."

Jill took a sip of her Riesling and nodded. "Wow, thanks for all your insight, J Mo. I had no idea I was exercising a well-known psychological principle. All this time, I just thought I was putting out a few small fires to try and slow down the big one."

Chris nodded at Jill's response and chimed in, "I'm blown away by your explanation. I understand how simple things can make a big difference, but I suppose it's easy to overlook the power that approach has in favor of valuing larger-scale systemic change all at once. People are more motivated by instant gratification, so the gratification of achieving small goals before the big, overarching one is brilliant, but I can see how it slips under the radar."

"Good workout today for both the body and mind," John said with a grin. J Mo slapped a hand on his thigh, standing up. "But now it's time to go to bed. Ladies, fellas—it has been a pleasure. And Jill, thank you for sharing your story with us tonight."

▨ ▨ ▨

"Of course," said Jill, also standing to leave. "I'm excited to hear somebody else's tomorrow."

Everyone said their goodnights as they walked toward the lodge and their cabins.

3

Turning Mundane Work into Exciting Work: Enhancing Work Engagement through Job Crafting

Day three turned out to be a cloudy day, and by nine o'clock that morning, it started to rain. The weather forecast indicated rain until 3:00 p.m. John, Kim, and Darnell were relieved, as there would be no hiking today. Sarah, Shawn, and Michael liked the hiking and were disappointed.

Dana arranged to screen the movie *Dances with Wolves* in the sitting room. She and Jean prepared a good lunch—no boxed lunches that day, as no one was going anywhere in the rain. The rain stopped by 4:00 p.m., but by then everyone had gone to their cabins, and most of them were content to stay there. But by 4:15 p.m., when the sun came out, Michael, Shawn, John, and Sarah decided to go for a walk in the woods.

As usual, after dinner, everyone gathered around the firepit. J Mo brought two bottles of WhistlePig, John's favorite whiskey. Jean dropped off a cooler filled with beer and Truly hard seltzer. Once everyone settled down with their beverages and the fire was roaring and warm, cushioned within what was a lovely evening after all the rain, J Mo asked, "Who is going to share their story next?"

Chris and Sarah raised their hands at the same time. They chuckled nervously for a second before Sarah waved her hand and said, "Chris, I can't wait to hear your story—so please start the evening with yours, and if there is time, I will share mine."

Chris agreed. He began by saying, "I want to take you back in time. Picture this: It is a beautiful sunny day. I am sitting in my office, overlooking an immaculate lawn, nibbling at my sandwich, even though I'm not hungry. I have a frown on my face and am feeling depressed.

"What happened, you ask? You see, I had recently applied for a promotion. My current job of department manager had prepared me well for the store manager job. I had worked in this role for seven years and was managing the largest and most profitable department of the store. I was the most qualified applicant for the position, but the job went to an outsider who had experience as a store manager of a much smaller store. Bottom line," he said, pausing for dramatic effect and taking a sip of his drink, "I did not get the job."

"I was obviously disappointed by that outcome, and I didn't know what to do with myself after the fact," he went on. "I had spent fifteen years with the company and had moved up the ranks. After seven years in the same job, I knew the job well. I was so good at my job that it was no longer challenging or interesting—it had become routine, and in fact, *boring*. Worse, without that specific promotion, I felt I had little chance of moving up in the organization. After all, Jennifer, the new store manager, had just arrived. She moved from Dallas, bought a house, and enrolled her children at the local elementary school. She was putting down roots and was likely to stay for a long time, which meant I could not become store manager as long as Jennifer held that job.

"Of course, there was the option of moving to another city if I really wanted to become a store manage—as the franchise has stores in every major city in the United States—but I didn't have the appetite to relocate. That would mean uprooting my family, which would make no one happy. My wife, Elaine, is a partner in a small boutique staffing company that specializes in placing employees in clerical and light manufacturing jobs with local employers. She and two of her college friends started the company twelve years ago and over the years grew their book of business. I realized Elaine's business success was the culmination of carefully developing ties with local businesses and earning their trust by placing productive and dependable employees. Moving would require Elaine to sell her business to her partners and start all over again. That simply wasn't realistic. Also, Melika, my fifteen-year-old daughter at the time, would have been devastated, as she had very close friendships with her classmates and was really excited about making the junior varsity softball team as a high school freshman. And Matthew, who had just turned eleven, had special needs. He has grown so much since then, but I'll never forget his bright smile at that age and his enthusiasm for all of the small things in life that others so easily overlook. It'd been hard to find him the guidance he needed in an educational setting, but we'd managed to find that in Cold Springs Elementary, and he was really thriving."

"It sounds like you would've sacrificed a lot to relocate," J Mo commented, and Chris shook his head grimly, sipping from his drink.

"*I* wouldn't have sacrificed anything—but my wife, daughter, and son would have sacrificed what mattered most to them. My desire for professional growth wasn't worth that cost. So, in short, I was feeling stuck. I had no immediate prospects to move up in the company, and my job had become routine and mundane. Yet, I understood the necessity of maintaining a positive attitude, because I did not want to take home my unhappiness and soil the home environment. I thought to myself, *How can I be happy, engaged, and productive at work when there aren't advancement opportunities and when the job has become routine and boring?*

"I resolved to make the most of the job I already had. I made a list of all the duties related to my current position and placed them into three categories: tasks that played to my strengths, tasks that aligned with my interests, and tasks I found unfulfilling. The latter category included mundane but important tasks, such as reviewing and recording inventory. I decided to delegate those to one of my subordinates, who was not only competent but aspired for a managerial position. I felt this would be a good development opportunity for her.

"I have a good analytical mind, and I am systematic in approaching tasks and problems. A second strength I have is my ability to relate with people. I am outgoing and socially adept. I was also interested in furthering my education—not in terms of getting an advanced degree, necessarily, but in terms of learning new skills and obtaining certifications. I like working with data. Gaining knowledge in data analytics seemed like a good way to combine my strengths and interests, so I enrolled in an online, six-months-long data analytics program offered by a local university. I felt such a program was suited to my situation, as I could spend a couple of hours in the evening working toward the certification. The first Saturday of each month, all the participants were expected to meet with each other and with faculty to learn aspects of data analytics and to get to know other participants in the program. I was looking forward to meeting like-minded individuals, socializing, and learning about their jobs and aspirations. Obtaining the certification would require passing three exams. I like working with data, am a disciplined individual, and am interested in learning, so that would not be a problem.

"By the time two months had passed since Jennifer was hired for the position I originally had my heart set on, we'd gotten to know each other better, and to tell you the truth, I was impressed with her," he said with a smile and a shake of his head. Everybody in the group grinned right along with him. "What can I say? She was a hard worker and was adapting well to managing a much larger store than she was used to. She also seemed genuinely interested in knowing all her managers. She knew I had applied for the store manager position, had been managing the largest department in the store, and was well-liked. She could have resented me and tried to marginalize me. Instead, she praised me for my contributions and explicitly acknowledged she would be depending on me to manage the store. She had me in her corner. To prove she was serious, Jennifer made me, unofficially, second-in-command. She also initiated a new project and requested me to serve as the project manager. The project involved studying the workflow of the store and suggesting changes that would increase its efficiency. I was enthusiastic about this expanded role and thought to himself, *Why didn't I think of this idea?*

"Although I knew everyone at the store, I only had a small circle of friends. To map the workflow of other departments and also get a grasp of how these other departments went about their duties, I set up meetings with each department. My goal was to meet with each department manager and a handful of employees who knew the department well. In all, I set up eleven meetings, one meeting per week. I felt having an initial two-hour meeting with each department to collect information, going back for clarification if needed, and developing a good grasp of the workflow in each department would take a few hours each week. Devoting a few hours per week to this new assignment was something

I could manage without feeling overwhelmed, as I still had to manage my department. These meetings transpired over three months, and in that time, I got to know more people and ended up forming close relationships with employees from almost every department. The project had the inadvertent effect of expanding my social circle, and it helped me form new friendships. As an extraverted person, I loved that.

"The first Saturday I attended in-person classes, I was a bit apprehensive, as I hadn't set foot on a college campus since I graduated college some twenty years ago. But I was eager to meet my classmates and learn what they did for a living. I was surprised to discover there were twenty-eight students enrolled in the program. For some reason, I was only expecting a dozen or so. To help students get acquainted with each other, the university had put together a class book that included photos of students along with a one-page bio, which was an edited version of what my fellow classmates and I had submitted when applying for the program.

"It was a full day—three hours of lectures and a one-hour lunch, followed by three hours of actual modeling and lab work. At 3:00 p.m., there would be a reception designed to create an opportunity for social interaction. As I ate my boxed lunch, I thumbed through the class book and identified a few people who seemed to be doing interesting work in bigger companies. I went looking for one of them—Julia, who worked as a logistics manager at a big transportation company. Julia was excited to be there and told me she was learning a lot of valuable knowledge she could apply to her job right away. Julia and I had a long conversation, exchanged contact information, and promised to stay in touch. I also met Roccio, who worked as data manager for a hospital. He too expressed enthusiasm about the program and how he could use modeling to engage in data mining for the hospital and track the flow of patients, reasons for hospital visits, and perhaps do some predictive modeling. I felt I had made the right decision enrolling in the program, although it wasn't yet clear to me how I might use the knowledge and skills from the program within my job at the store.

"The project to map the store's workflow was coming along nicely, and I was pleased with the progress. I spent evenings working on the project; I didn't mind, as it was interesting work. As I was working on the report, I noticed I was fully absorbed in the writing, and time seemed to fly by. Finally, the report was done. Now, all I had to do was make a presentation to Jennifer and all the department managers. I put together a few PowerPoint slides and felt ready. Jennifer was extremely pleased with my report and the presentation, and we all, including the department managers, could see how altering workflow in some areas could save time by reducing work for employees. It was a success.

"The data analytics program came to an end six months later, and I ended up passing my certification exams. I took my wife to the graduation ceremony and introduced her to Julia, Roccio, and a few others. I felt such a sense of accomplishment and was as happy as a kid in a candy store.

"The next morning, as I was driving to work, I reflected on the last nine months. When Jennifer was hired for the store manager job—or, more precisely, when I was *not* hired for the store manager job—I was extremely disappointed and depressed, because I was certain there wasn't any other way to advance within the company; I felt my job was pretty much a dead-end job. But things had changed so much for me in only nine months!" Chris looked around the circle of new friends again, a broad smile on his face. "I had developed new skills," he went on, counting each point made by holding up a finger, "expanded my social network both at work and outside of work, and had just completed an interesting and useful project for the company that was well received by my new supervisor. I had converted a boring job into an exciting job. I loved my current position; I was fully engrossed in it to the degree that time seemed to pass quickly, and I felt the job was really rewarding."

"Good for you, Chris," Jill said, raising her Riesling.

He nodded at her, raising his own glass, and continued. "A few weeks later, I went into work and found Jennifer waiting for me in my office. She motioned for me to join her in her office." He paused then, swallowing. "I was nervous, honestly, because this meeting was unannounced, and I wasn't at all sure what she'd need to talk to me privately about. But then, with a big smile, she said, 'Chris, I just obtained authorization to promote you to an assistant store manager position. You know, ours is one of the largest stores in the franchise, and given your capabilities, you will be able to make a storewide impact, just as you have done with the workflow project.' Jennifer had lobbied for and created a new position—assistant store manager—just for me. Nationally, only three other stores had such a position. I was beyond delighted. I now fully understand my mother's phrase, 'Only you control your happiness and your success.'"

"Wow, what a remarkable journey you've had, my friend," said Darnell. "It's so positive and uplifting. I think it's good for us all to reflect less on the power we *do not* have and more on the power we *do* have over our current circumstances."

※　※　※

Jill nodded and said, "Instead of falling into a downward spiral, you completely turned around your work life. You are a remarkable man."

"Well done, Chris," J Mo echoed. "You are a fighter."

Shawn shifted his weight in his chair, eyeing J Mo with a grin. "Go ahead, J Mo. Please offer your insights—we're all waiting to hear what you've got to say on this one. What did Chris experience and what theory or theories can be used to understand why the actions Chris took worked?"

UNDERLYING THEORETICAL FRAMEWORK

J Mo took a sip of his whiskey before launching into his thoughts. "There are three theoretical perspectives that can be used to answer your questions, Shawn. First, more than ever, the work environment is constantly changing due to increased competition, technological advancements, and globalization. Consequently, to stay competitive, companies have downsized their management tiers—meaning fewer managers now supervise and oversee more subordinates than ever before. This downsizing has diminished advancement opportunities in management positions, leading to what is called *hierarchical plateaus.* A hierarchical plateau is the point in a career at which the likelihood of advancement is very low. In turn, fewer promotional opportunities result in employees staying in their existing positions for much longer periods of time, contributing to *job content plateaus.* Now, a job content plateau is the perception that one's job is no longer challenging or interesting, that it has become routine, mundane, or boring.

"From what I've gleaned, it seems the organizational structure of Chris's store was flat, with only three levels of management: section managers who reported to department managers who, in turn, reported to the store manager. It took Chris eight years to become a department manager. He had seven years of experience as a department manager when he applied to become the store manager. Because he did not get the job and there were no more promotion opportunities for him, he experienced hierarchical plateau. And, since the job was no longer challenging, it wasn't intrinsically motivating, so he also experienced job content plateau. Perceiving a lack of advancement opportunities and realizing one's job is no longer interesting has negative performance and health consequences.

"But instead of giving up, Chris turned life around. How?" J Mo said, looking at everyone in the group. They remained silent, waiting for his answer. "Chris engaged in what is called *job crafting*. Job crafting refers to self-initiated, proactive strategies to change work characteristics to better align one's job with personal needs, goals, and skills. Individual employees can self-initiate changes to the type and scope of tasks they conduct at work, the quality or frequency of interaction with others at work, and the way they cognitively frame or view their job.

"So, how is job crafting achieved? Job crafting can be achieved through increasing structural resources, such as autonomy or pursuing developmental opportunities; increasing social resources, such as social support or developing quality social relationships; increasing challenging job demands, such as taking on additional responsibilities or taking on new projects that are stimulating as opposed to hindering; and lastly, decreasing hindering job demands, such as tasks that are not motivational but drain resources.

   ▦   ▦   ▦

"A related theoretical framework organizes job crafting as follows: one, *approach crafting*, which involves initiatives such as taking on extra tasks, developing skills and abilities, and upgrading qualifications; two, *relational crafting*, which involves things like actively developing relationships at work and creating new relationships; and three, cognitively reframing qualities at work, such as reframing one's role and focusing on the positive impact of one's job.

"Chris completed the data analytics program, thereby developing new skills and increasing his structural resources. Thus, he engaged in approach crafting. Second, when working on the workflow project, he was able to develop new social connections—and the same could be said for the time he spent completing the data analytics program, where he made important social connections with fellow classmates. By engaging in such relational crafting, Chris was able to increase his social resources."

Darnell raised his hand the way a student might in class, and everybody in the group chuckled at his humor. J Mo played along by saying, "Yes, Darnell? Do you have a question?"

Can I ask what social resources are?" Darnell asked, putting his hand down.

J Mo replied, "Social resources contribute to social capital—and the more social capital you have, the better you will be able to leverage your human capital to achieve success." Then, returning to his original list, he said, "So, third, by taking on the workflow project, Chris increased challenging job demands, another example of approach crafting. Finally, he was able to reduce hindering job demands by giving away routine, nonmotivational tasks to aspiring managers. In this way, Chris engaged in job crafting to make his job more motivating, interesting, and rewarding."

"Are there any consequences to job crafting?" Jill asked.

"I'm glad you asked, Jill," J Mo replied. "By engaging in job crafting, Chris was able to enhance his work engagement. Work engagement, the third theoretical concept, refers to a positive, fulfilling, work-related state of mind that is characterized by vigor, dedication, and absorption. *Vigor* is characterized by high levels of energy and mental resilience while working. *Dedication* refers to being strongly involved in one's work and experiencing a sense of significance, enthusiasm, and challenge. Finally, *absorption* is characterized by being fully concentrated and happily engrossed in one's work. When absorbed in one's work, time tends to pass quickly, and people can even find it challenging to detach from their work life." J Mo paused for a moment, collecting his thoughts before adding, "In essence, work engagement captures how workers *experience* their work. Engaged employees have an energetic and affective connection with their work activities with raised motivation. Employees who engage in job crafting behavior proactively try to align their work tasks to their own strengths, interests, and developmental aspirations. By doing so, they create a challenging and fitting work environment that fosters the enthusiasm and absorption characteristic of work engagement. Through job crafting, Chris was able to turn his mundane job into a more enriched job, and through this transformation, he was able to enhance his work engagement. He felt reinvigorated at work, was dedicated to his transformed job, and was fully absorbed in the job—so much so that time seemed to fly by, which is also known as *experiencing a state of flow.* Basketball players call it being *in the zone.*

■   ■   ■

"Engaged employees experience performance benefits of all kinds, such as higher performance evaluations, higher ratings of promotability, and promotions. Another benefit of feeling fulfilled by one's job has to do with one's health, such as psychological well-being. A side benefit of work engagement is that it has the potential to buffer the negative effects of stressors, such as work overload or role conflict on strain."

How to Apply These Ideas to Achieve Success

"Now," J Mo continued, "how can we apply these ideas to achieve both personal and professional success for ourselves the way Chris did? If you find yourself in a job that is no longer challenging, consider job crafting. First, do what Chris did and classify your job duties into three categories: tasks that fit your strengths, tasks that fit your interests, and tasks that you no longer wish to perform. Second, if possible, delegate tasks you no longer wish to perform to a subordinate. If you don't have a subordinate, trade tasks with a coworker in exchange for something you find interesting. Third, engage in approach crafting by increasing structural resources and challenging job demands. Fourth, engage in relational crafting by seeking ways to increase your social resources.

"Over time, you will transform your mundane job into one that is intrinsically motivating and experience vigor, dedication, and absorption, thereby increasing your work engagement. Thus, job crafting will help you lower perceptions of hierarchical and job content plateaus and increase your work engagement, so your job is intrinsically rewarding, motivating, and meaningful. And you may even be rewarded with a promotion, just as Chris was."

In What Situations Will Implementing These Ideas Be Most Effective?

"To compete in this dynamic environment," J Mo went on, "organizations are tightening their belts, so to speak, by delayering—or downsizing management positions—and streamlining all business operations to as few supervisors as possible. Consequently, there will be fewer promotional opportunities for everybody else, which means you will stay in your current job longer. Most of us will experience hierarchical plateau at some point in life, and perhaps even job content plateau at least once or several times throughout our careers. As we've discussed, perceiving hierarchical and job content plateaus will negatively affect our performance and psychological well-being, and if you don't do anything to change the situation, you will most likely find yourself in a downward spiral, and things will get worse and worse.

"If you find yourself in this situation, you could also move laterally within the organization, if possible, to alleviate job content plateau—but you will still have to contend with hierarchical plateau. Alternatively, you could use the job crafting ideas we talked about earlier to turn things around and experience increased work engagement. Of course, you don't have to wait until you experience these plateaus to engage in job crafting. The best advice would be to routinely use these ideas to continuously craft your job so it is always exciting and intrinsically motivating, which will enable you to be fully engaged in your work.

"Your job might be such that you can initiate and sustain job crafting without consulting with your supervisor, but that is unlikely to be the case for most of us. In such situations, it is best to consult with, involve, and gain the support of your supervisor before embarking on your job crafting journey."

With J Mo's spiel finished, everyone congratulated Chris on his success. John called him a role model. Jill and Sarah appreciated the fact that he put his family's interests before his own by deciding against relocating and instead working hard to convert a bad situation into a good one. Chris was blushing, and in the effort of redirecting attention away from him, he nodded to Sarah and said, "Sarah, are you going next?"

"You know what? I think I will. But I need a bathroom break first," Sarah replied, and everybody mumbled their agreement. The group took a brief break before returning to the firepit.

4

Enhancing Career Success through Career Adaptability and Proactive Behaviors

With drinks in hand, everyone gathered around the firepit, eager to hear Sarah's journey. She kicked things off by saying, "Interestingly enough, my story shares a few similarities to Chris's, in that it has to do with being proactive and adaptable to achieve your goals. But I'm going to approach this differently. First, let me tell you where I am right now in my career, and then I'll share with you how I got there.

"Two weeks ago, I accepted a new job. When Troy, my supervisor, called to offer me the job, I was smiling so much my face hurt. So, as of now, in three weeks, I'll be starting my new job as vice president of data and information security at a Fortune 500 company."

The group broke out in smiles and applause, a few people even saying, "Congratulations!"

Michael looked Sarah up and down, clearly impressed. "Wow! What a huge accomplishment for somebody your age, if you don't mind me saying."

Sarah nodded at Michael and replied, "A colleauge told me I'm the youngest person ever to hold such a high-level position in this company, but I've never fact-checked that."

"Can we ask how old you are, Sarah?" Jill asked. "If that's too personal, forget I asked."

"I'm only in my thirties," Sarah replied with a smile. "I graduated from college just over a decade ago, and it's my goal to become a CEO of a Fortune 500 company by the time I'm forty-five. I feel confident about achieving that—I can feel it in my bones."

"At the rate you're going, I have no doubt you will become a CEO by then," Jill said with raised brows. "I am so impressed!"

Michael shook his head and said, "After that, you should run for president of the United States!"

Everybody laughed, including Sarah, who then went on to say, "Now that I've told you where I am and what my goals are, let me start from the beginning. I grew up in a loving family with two older brothers, one who is two years older than me and one who is five years older than me. They were my guardian angels, and I admired them. I hung out more with Mason than with Jackson, as Mason was closer to my age. I would jokingly introduce Mason as my little older brother.

"My dad served in the military for thirty years and retired as a lieutenant colonel. He had an engineering background and had graduated from West Point. He was a hard worker, dedicated to his craft. During his career, he was deployed several times, including to Afghanistan to oversee major projects, such as building barracks, roads, and headquarters for the US Army, as well as several projects for Afghan agencies. At one point, he was responsible for nearly fifty projects worth $450 million. My dad always used to say, 'There is no limit to what you can achieve if you put your mind to the task,' and that statement has stuck with me.

"Growing up was a fun but also very challenging for me and my brothers. As a military family, we moved every two to three years, leaving behind friends, classmates, and neighbors. Before I went to the University of Michigan, my family had moved so many times that my brothers and I had ended up attending seven different schools. It was tough for my mother to hold a steady job. After the third move, she became a free-lancer, developing marketing materials or copyediting and proofing such materials for various companies. She had her own website, so it did not matter if the family moved. Over time, she built a loyal clientele.

"When I was younger, I would cry every time we moved. My brothers would make fun of me, and my mother would say, 'Sarah, new adventures await you.' One constant companion for me was my imagination, and I loved to engage in playing pretend. One day, I would dress up as a nurse and play nurse the whole day. My poor brothers had to pretend they had different ailments, and I would treat them and instruct them what they could do and could not do. Mason did not like this much, but Jackson was a trooper and would play along. The next day, I would be a firefighter; the following day, a policeman; the next, a doctor. I persuaded my mother to help me make appropriate costumes to make my pretend play more realistic. I just had a vivid imagination.

"As I got older, I began to view each move as an opportunity to explore new environments and to make new friends and new memories. Our family ended up living on five different army bases and in one midsized town. I loved living on bases. Although there were similarities between bases, somehow each had its own unique culture. I would write down the similarities and differences between the current and previous base and discuss them with my brothers to validate my perceptions. My brothers hated it, but I loved the analyzing and debating.

"With every move, I became better at making friends and forming social connections. I was smart and could easily adapt to the curriculum of the new school. My favorite move, though, was when we lived in South Korea for three years when I was in middle school. I enjoyed all the attention from Korean students and their families. I was curious about the Korean culture and language, and with the help of a tutor, I learned Korean. By the time we left Korea to return to the US, I could read, write, and speak the language fluently. I liked learning about different cultures; in fact, I would embed myself in the local culture so much that no one would believe I had only recently moved to the area. I had developed an almost chameleon-like ability to adapt. My brothers would jokingly call me Cami. Even with all the moves, I kept up my grades. I had a good work ethic, always worked hard, and believed I controlled my own destiny.

"I graduated high school with an unweighted GPA of 4.0. With an ACT score of 35 and participation in many extracurricular activities, I received admission letters from half a dozen schools, and I ultimately chose to attend the University of Michigan, Jackson's alma mater. But unlike my brother, who studied accounting, I was passionate about computer science. You see, I had spent the last two summers attending coding camps, was already proficient in C++ and Java programming, and enjoyed working with numbers. My aptitude for math led me to pursue programming. I ended up majoring in computer science with a concentration in data analytics. I also minored in Korean because of my passion for the Korean language and culture. The summer after my freshman year, I interned with a financial services company. I went back to the same company the following summer. The summer after my junior year, I interned with the Michigan Department of Transportation. Although I did interesting work there, I decided to work for a for-profit organization upon graduation.

"I graduated summa cum laude from Michigan—which was not an easy feat, given the rigor of the curriculum—and I received offers from four companies to work as a data analyst. I did my homework; I studied each offer's industry to determine if it was growing and whether the company was on the growth trajectory, and I tried to find out as much as I could about career prospects within the company. Two months later, I started my first job. It was an exciting time for me; I liked my boss and most of my coworkers.

"It only took me six months to master my job. While some tasks required a higher level of competency, I was a quick study and had no qualms with working late or working an occasional weekend to finish the job. My boss was impressed with my technical knowledge, dedication, open-mindedness, and willingness to help other coworkers with their projects. A year passed, and I was comfortable with my job, enjoyed interacting with my coworkers, and was very pleased to receive outstanding performance evaluations. My boss said, 'You are already among the best, if not the best, data analyst in this company,' which made me feel really good about myself and what I was doing.

"I enjoyed attending the monthly lunch meetings of the local Data Analytics Association, as it afforded me the opportunity to meet other data analysts, senior managers, and aspiring data analysts. I made it a point to sit at a different table at each meeting, so I could meet more people. I would always follow up with people I met, attempting to forge quality relationships with senior managers and learn from more experienced data analysts. I also joined the National Data Analytics Association. At any one time, the association had several task forces, each charged with investigating a topic. The findings of the task forces would then be distributed via their monthly magazine sent to members of the association. I volunteered to serve on a task force charged with reviewing the latest data mining techniques, and it ended up being a great experience for me. My curious nature enabled me to learn about the types of questions being addressed at different organizations and explore career opportunities at those organizations.

"In working with a group of experts employed at organizations across the country, I learned as much as I contributed to the task force. Through conversations with others, I found out many of the members of the task force had advanced degrees or certifications, so I realized that to be competitive in the industry marketplace, I would have to either pursue an advanced degree, additional certifications, or both.

"After an extensive search process and many conversations with experts, I chose to pursue a master's degree in computer science with a concentration in data analytics. I then enrolled in an online program offered by MIT. I chose that particular university because students completing the program would not only be awarded a master's degree but would also be awarded a graduate-level certificate in data analytics—the highest certification available in the discipline.

"The next two years were very busy for me, as balancing a full-time job with graduate studies was challenging. Although I had to sacrifice my social life, I loved to learn, and I was motivated to excel in the program because it was my best shot at ensuring career opportunities in the future. I felt additional education would help me master the subject and shape my career trajectory. My goal was not just to become skilled in data analytics but to become an *expert*. I remembered what my father used to say: 'There is no limit to what you can achieve if you put your mind to the task.' I believed in that philosophy all the more as I pursued my studies.

"With every class, my confidence grew. I was learning new, advanced skills and was constantly discussing ways to use my advanced knowledge to the advantage of the company. In addition, I could ask more sophisticated questions that would lead to improving the overall efficiency of the whole organization. My boss was excited about my suggestions and empowered me to use my talents fully. I took on increasingly challenging projects, and my contributions were noticed by senior executives in the organization. A week before I completed my master's degree, I was promoted to the senior data analyst position, and I became my boss's right hand.

"I realized that like most companies, ours was data rich but insight poor, and I was determined to change that. My job then was to work with my boss to develop and assign projects to other data analysts in the organization. I would then help the other data analysts complete projects by providing guidance and mentorship and troubleshooting as needed.

"Slowly but surely, the CIO started noticing the contributions of the data analytics unit. The insights offered by the unit were informing important business decisions—especially in the areas of marketing—and were improving efficacy in the operation of the organization. In recognition, the CIO promoted my boss and made him one of his direct reports, so he could more effectively leverage the unit's contribution. My boss and the CIO appreciated my expertise and rewarded me with a huge raise.

"Over the next five years, I made a name for myself with the national association. I was elected to serve as chair of the programming committee. The charge of the committee was to develop and offer online programming on important topics to the membership. I was emerging as one of the leading experts in the field and was beginning to be recognized as such. I was not only gaining knowledge and expertise but pushing the boundaries of the field by developing new approaches and algorithms for data mining. I am passionate about my work, and the recognition as an expert boosted my confidence in my ability to discern trends in the data, and translate them into business decisions.

"Over the last several years, I have become interested in security issues, so I enrolled in an online information security program, and after the program ended, I passed the Certified Information Systems Security Professional (CISSP) certification.

"Things were going extremely well for me until the company I worked for was taken over by another company and all the employees in my department were laid off. I went from having a great job to having to look for a new one. There were more job openings in the information security space than in the data analytics space, so I applied for and was hired as a director of information security at a privately held wealth management company. I reported directly to the chief information officer. I worked as director for a few years. I have learned so much about security issues that I can honestly call myself a security expert.

"A few weeks ago, my whole family came to my condo to celebrate my birthday. I felt blessed and lucky. A week later, I was approached by a headhunter. This wasn't new, but this time, it was different. The headhunter asked if I would be interested in working for a Fortune 500 company as the vice president of data and information security, reporting directly to the CIO." Sarah paused, looking at the group with a smile. "How could I say no?"

"Sarah, you are remarkable person," said Jill.

Michael nodded in agreement. "I don't mean to offend anyone, but I think you might be the most successful individual in this group."

Everyone chuckled, and a few said, "Agreed!"

Shawn added, "I am convinced you will become a CEO of a Fortune 500 company soon—and when that happens, hire me, please."

"Sarah," J Mo chimed in, "you are among the most successful people I have ever met."

"Thanks, J Mo," she said, blushing slightly. "I am so eager to listen to your analysis. I think I know why I'm successful, but I'd like to hear your insights, as I've already learned so much from you."

J Mo studied her for a moment. "Why do *you* think you're successful?"

"Well, I'm smart, I work hard, I had a good boss, and I was at the right place at the right time."

"True," said J Mo. "But that's not all. Here is my perspective . . ."

UNDERLYING THEORETICAL FRAMEWORK

"Let me begin by setting the context," said J Mo. "As I'm sure all of you know, the business and corporate landscape is always changing. This has run predictable career trajectories virtually into extinction, leaving it up to the individual to take control of their career development. Now, as a result, self-directed and customizable career paths have gained preference among most people and personal resources are becoming more relevant to successful career development.

"This takes us to what is called *career adaptability*, which is one of the core components of vocational psychology and career construction theory. Career adaptability can be defined as a psychosocial construct that denotes an individual's resources for coping with current and anticipated tasks, transitions, and traumas in their occupational roles.'" J Mo paused, as though waiting for the group to take notes, before adding, "Now, career adaptability has four components: concern about the future, or *planning;* control over life, or *decision-making;* curiosity about occupational careers, or *being inquisitive;* and confidence to construct a future and deal with career barriers, or *problem-solving.*

"Career construction theory posits that individuals differ in their adaptivity and ability to engage in positive career-related behaviors. These adapting behaviors, in turn, allow for the successful integration of the self into the work role—or, in other words, adaptation results.

"Adaptivity, or adaptive readiness, is the personality trait of flexibility or willingness to change. Adaptability resources—such as concern, control, curiosity, and confidence—can be drawn on to help individuals cope with current or anticipated change. These adaptivity resources are behaviors that equip an individual with the ability to positively embrace spontaneous change, resulting in *adaptation*, the key word here.

"As a future-focused dimension of career adaptability, *concern* refers to the extent an individual is opportunity-oriented, possess career-related forethought, and prepares for upcoming career challenges. Individuals who score high on concern are likely to think about and prepare for their vocational future, including carefully planning how to achieve their career goals. The realization of such goals is facilitated by an awareness of how contemporaneous choices and opportunities—such as the decision to obtain further education or training in one's field to encourage career advancement—influences this process.

"*Control* empowers people to feel responsible for shaping their career. It entails a strong self-determination component, enables individuals to become responsible for influencing themselves and their environment, and thus reflects mastery over the environment. Control also manifests as positivity, self-directed decision-making, responsibility, self-efficacy, and striving toward self-preservation.

"*Curiosity*, on the other hand, is more of an indicator of vocational inquisitiveness and the propensity to engage in opportunity-focused, career-related activities. It motivates the individual to explore alternative routes in the scope of their career, leading to the ability to augment the less desirable attributes of their vocational life as needed or desired."

"So," Chris interjected, "sort of like what I did when I faced hierarchy plateau—I used my sense of curiosity to reinvent my career, augmenting whatever I could to get me closer to a role within the company that I desired most."

"Exactly," J Mo answered, smiling. Then he nodded at Jill. "And I would use Jill as an example of the control component—she used her own self-direction and decision-making to reshape what her job was capable of achieving. But before we get into all that, let's get back to curiosity.

"Curiosity involves exploring possible future selves and associated career prospects and thinking about how such opportunities may influence different work roles and environments. This way of perceiving things also means adopting an exploratory attitude toward different or even unusual career options by investigating their surroundings and seeking opportunities to grow.

"Now, on to our last career adaptability resource: confidence. This refers to an individual's belief in themselves and their ability to attain their career goals—and it is quite similar to the concept we talked about a few days ago, self-efficacy. Confidence reflects the degree of self-efficacy one has to pursue their vocational aspirations, solve the problems they encounter, and succeed in the face of adversity. Confident people tend to perform tasks more efficiently and take care to do so well. Confidence is likewise associated with a desire to learn new skills and demonstrate abilities. Higher capacities for problem-solving and overcoming obstacles are also characteristics of confident individuals.

How Do You Develop High Levels of Career Adaptability?

"All of those aspects combined create career adaptability, which is sort of like a superpower in the realm of vocational success." J Mo gestured to Sarah and said, "Sarah is a great example of what career adaptability looks like. So, how did she use this adaptability, specifically, to succeed the way she has? Growing up in a loving family and developing a healthy relationship with siblings contributed to her becoming a socially well-adjusted individual, I'd argue. The frequent moves of her family enhanced her adaptive readiness—a willingness to learn, grow, and adapt. Experiences with successfully adapting to new environments contributed to her overall adaptability.

"More specifically, she developed her curiosity from a young age. Engaging in pretend play—playing a nurse, a firefighter, a policeman, a doctor—allowed her to imagine herself in different roles, nurturing her innate desire to explore and compare different possible selves. In addition, whenever the family relocated, she would begin making inquiries about clubs at school and local sports teams to carefully decide how best to allocate her time and energy. She was curious to examine how the current military base differed from the previous one and would systematically compare and contrast those experiences. When she was offered multiple jobs, she gathered as much information as possible about each job offer and the company to carefully select the offer that would most benefit her career.

"Her curiosity led her to exercise control. When the family relocated to South Korea, she took the opportunity to learn the language and embed herself in the Korean culture. In high school, she took control of her future by attending coding boot camps to prepare herself for her vocation. Likewise, when attending the University of Michigan, she completed three internships to prepare herself for her vocational future.

* * *

"Sarah, despite the frequent moves, was smart, hardworking, and always earned good grades. She controlled her destiny and was often reminded by her dad that 'there is no limit to what you can achieve if you put your mind to the task.' She also learned from her mother, who took control of her life by launching a career as a freelancer.

"Sarah's confidence in herself was the result of her accumulated accomplishments, her ability to easily make new friends, her open-mindedness, and her ability to adjust remarkably well to new environments. She excelled at school, aced her ACT, and had impressive credentials to get into a top school. Her coding experience during high school and graduating summa cum laude from Michigan boosted her confidence in her ability to achieve her goals. Collectively, these experiences contributed to her high level of adaptability, which helped her in her career.

Influence of Career Adaptability on Career Success

"From an early age, Sarah developed her adaptability, which helped her adapt to her first job. Her curiosity, her desire to be in control, her concern for her career, and her confidence in her abilities helped her navigate the job environment and master her job tasks. From her first day in the work world, she exhibited her curiosity by joining local and national data analytics associations, meeting people, forming connections, volunteering to serve on task forces of the national organization, and later chairing the programming committee to develop new training and development opportunities for the membership of the national association. These initiatives enabled her to explore and learn about options that could help her career.

"Her concern for her career led her to believe an advanced education was necessary to equip herself with knowledge and skills needed to meet future challenges. She acted on this belief and took control by enrolling in a master's program. She completed the program and along the way, secured a graduate-level certification, the highest academic qualification in the discipline. This ensured she was technically competent. Her drive to excel and previous successes boosted her confidence.

"She was then willing to ask more sophisticated questions and develop new techniques and algorithms for data mining. The positive contributions she was able to make to the organization led to increases in salary and promotion. Establishing herself as a thought leader in the field helped her get noticed at a national level. When she was laid off, her training and skills in information security came in handy, and she adapted to switching from doing data analytics work to data and information security work with ease. Her education, certifications, experiences, and recognition at the national level resulted in the job offer from a Fortune 500 company to work as VP of data and information security, contributing to her career success."

How to Apply These Ideas to Achieve Success

"This is great and all," Darnell interjected, "but what about those of us who don't inherently have the components of career adaptability? How would we go about gaining a sense of concern, control, curiosity, and confidence?"

■   ■   ■

"The good news, Darnell, is that career adaptability is a *malleable construct*, which means you can work to improve it," J Mo replied. "To enhance your career adaptability, be willing to explore, learn, grow, change, and adapt. Second, develop your curiosity and explore different vocational possibilities. Third, be concerned about your future, recognize and take advantage of developmental opportunities. Fourth, take control by engaging in upskilling. Finally, be confident, believe in your capabilities. These proactive career behaviors will help in planning and acquiring competencies, setting you up well to thrive in changing environments and achieve career success."

In What Situations Will Implementing These Ideas Be Most Effective?

"In contemporary work organizations, you are responsible for shaping your career. While some organizations have career ladders outlined, the ultimate responsibility for charting your career path is yours. In fact, the best advice would be to continuously use these ideas to further your career or put yourself in a position where you can take advantage of opportunities as they come along or create new opportunities for yourself."

"Wow, what an analysis. This is extremely insightful," said Chris.

Sarah commented, "In a million years, I would not have truly realized why I was successful. Thank you so much, J Mo!"

"Spending money for this camp may be the best investment I have ever made, and I bought ten thousand shares of Facebook at $40 per share," said Shawn.

J Mo smiled and said, "I am enjoying this camp as much as all of you—so, thank you for coming."

CHAPTER

5

Enhancing Reputation through Political Skill

Day four was sunny with a cool breeze and a forecasted high of eighty-five degrees, a perfect day for outdoor activities. As usual, Dana and Jean prepared a hearty breakfast of oatmeal, cereal, assorted fruits, croissants, muffins, and made-to-order omelets. Everyone assembled in the sitting room by 9:20 that morning. It seemed like a day of rest had rejuvenated the group, and they were ready to go. Dana passed around their backpacks packed with lunch, water, and snacks.

J Mo and the group hiked to a place that had several smaller in-terconnected lakes. It took them two hours to get to the lakes, and it was already lunchtime when they arrived. After eating their boxed lunches and taking a brief rest break, they got into canoes—two to a canoe—and started paddling through the narrow, winding lakes. The forest was so overgrown that most of the time they were covered by a canopy. They gathered near the shallow end of one of the lakes and started to fish. Only Michael caught a few fish, but they were small and were thus released back into the lake. After spending the day relaxing in canoes, under a canopy of giant trees, the group headed back to the cabin and saw some deer and coyotes along the way.

Dana and Jean prepared an excellent dinner, and the main dish was the fish they had caught two days earlier. Lightly battered and fried or grilled, the choice was theirs. J Mo found some bottles of wine that went well with fish. Everyone enjoyed the dinner, and they were gathered around the firepit well before 8:00 p.m. J Mo stood in front the lodge, a good fifty yards away from the firepit, and listened to the group's friendly banter and laughter. He thought to himself, *The group is really coming together and forming new friendships. It's remarkable how well these eight strangers are getting along.*

As soon as J Mo arrived at the fire, Shawn raised his hand and said, "Can I share my story tonight?"

"By all means," J Mo said, along with the encouragement of everybody else in the group.

Shawn took a deep breath before launching into his career journey story. "I hate to follow Sarah, but here I go. I'm going to follow Sarah's lead of telling you where I am now and then sharing how I got here.

"I am the general manager of the largest engineering firm in India. I want to note that in India, the general manager is the equivalent of the United States CEO. My engineering firm is well-known in the industry and is a subsidiary of the global giant Custom Works, headquartered in Chicago, Illinois. I enjoy visiting Chicago, and I am looking forward to seeing my peers and senior staff of the company at the quarterly meeting in two weeks.

Sarah interjected, saying, "Shawn, next time you're in Chicago, let me know, and we can grab dinner and drinks."

"Absolutely, I will," Shawn said, before continuing to tell his story. "As you probably guessed by now, I grew up in India—Madras, which is now called Chennai, to be exact—along with my younger brother, Zach. My dad worked as a marketing manager for a pharmaceutical company. He spent his entire career in sales and marketing. My mom is a homemaker. My family was a middle-class family, and I grew up in a two-bedroom rental house that was attached to other similar units, much like condominiums in the US. The living space was tight, as my grandmother, uncle, and aunt also lived in the same house. My dad, as the eldest son, had to care for his mother and unmarried younger siblings. My mom truly cared for my dad's family and treated my grandma, uncle, and aunty as if they were her own mother and siblings.

"One room served as a bedroom for my mom and dad, and my brother's and my stuff was stored in that room. The family room had closets to store the personal belongings of my grandma, uncle, and aunty, and there was space left for a dining table, a TV, and a couple of chairs. The other room served as the visitors' room to entertain guests and had two sofas and a coffee table.

"Even though our family lived paycheck to paycheck, my parents knew the value of a good education and sent my brother and me to a private school. The private school was quite expensive, but the teachers were competent, maintained high standards, expected students to work hard, and generally prepared them well for higher education. My brother and I excelled at school and finished every year at the top of the class. In every class, every year, students would be ranked, and we would always finish in the top three; any rank less than three would be a disaster, akin to failing.

"I vividly remember some of the rituals from my school days. Every year, the school would administer quarterly exams, half-yearly exams, and final exams. The school would send report cards home with students, and students were required to get theirs signed by a parent. I would show my report card to dad, who would say, 'Show it to Mom.' My mom knew her numbers but could not read or write in English, only her native Tamil. She would ask me to read the report card, and I would read: English, ninety-one points; Tamil, eighty-five points; math, ninety-eight points; science, ninety-six points; and so on. She would stop me and ask why I only got ninety-eight points in math and only ninety-six points in science. Then she would say, 'The teacher doesn't need the two points in math or the four points in science—*you* do. Next time, you need to get a hundred percent in both subjects.' She would decline to sign the report card to show her unhappiness. But eventually, after some pleading, I would get her to sign it. Often, she would make us sit down and tell us, 'Your only ticket to a better future is your education; we have nothing else to give you.' She would almost tear up every time and hug us.

"I got lucky, I guess. I was bright, grasped ideas quickly, and could remember information well, so I didn't have to study hard to excel in school. My classmates would often come to see me hours before an exam to ask me questions about concepts they did not understand or to clarify any confusion they had on a certain subject. I would patiently explain the concepts and provide examples to illustrate ideas, which they appreciated.

"In each grade—grades five through eleven—I was elected as the class leader. In twelfth grade, I was elected to serve as the school pupil leader, which was akin to the president of student body in American high schools. I not only excelled in academics but played cricket, played soccer, and ran track. Long jump was my favorite event. My school had a decent cricket team; I was an all-rounder, meaning I was good at both batting and bowling. During the cricket season, my team would play a match every Saturday against other local high school teams. Most everyone at the high school knew me, and I knew everyone; in fact, I knew at least one personal thing about each student because I cared for others and was genuine in my interactions. When a classmate of mine lost his father in a car accident, the entire school was devasted. The classmate, Sunil, had a younger sister, and his mother, Sangeeta, was a homemaker—even though she had a bachelor's degree in commerce, which is the equivalent of an accounting degree in the US. I wanted to do something, so I quickly organized a series of fundraisers, energized the entire student body to help, and raised enough money to pay all their household expenses for an entire year. I also talked to another classmate whose dad owned a big factory and secured Sangeeta a job as an accountant. The school principal told me he was impressed with my compassion and my ability to get things done. As school pupil leader, I organized and successfully executed several other volunteer activities and fundraisers to benefit local nonprofit organizations, such as the suicide prevention center, the homeless shelter, and the community food pantry. Because I was well-connected, genuine, and could discern the pulse of the student body, I knew what to say and how to say it to elicit commitment from others.

"I learned how to relate to people by observing my dad interact with others, especially with his sales team members. Nearly a dozen sales representatives reported to my dad. In India, there is virtually no work-life balance, and it wasn't uncommon for his subordinates to stop by the house, unannounced—just like the pop-ins from *Seinfeld*. Pretty much every other evening and on weekends, sales reps would show up at the house to discuss business. Four or five of them would sit shoulder to shoulder on the sofas, my dad would sit in his chair, and I would drag a stool from the family room to the visitors' room and sit in a corner. My dad and few of his subordinates smoked cigarettes, and my job was to empty ashtrays every now and then so they wouldn't overflow. And, when my mom called, I would hurry into the kitchen and bring a tray filled with cups of tea and serve the guests. My mom made special tea by boiling milk and water, then adding tea powder, letting it boil to the right temperature, and then adding sugar to it. It was simply delicious, and I would get to drink half a cup of it. It was a treat.

"I would sit on the stool and observe how my dad related to his subordinates. My dad was always polite, cordial, and respectful. He treated them like equals. Sales reps had to meet monthly sales targets and would get anxious when they weren't on track to achieve those targets, but my dad would never tell them what they needed to do better in order to meet those quotas. Instead, he would ask them questions, which led to brainstorming and strategizing. The sales reps would walk out feeling inspired to meet their quotas rather than feeling powerless. My dad was skillful in leading his subordinates and embedding ideas in the conversation so they learned how to think, ask questions, and come up with solutions all on their own.

"I paid attention to what my father was saying and how he was saying it, studying the nuances and charisma behind how he influenced others. It came naturally to my dad, but for me it was learned behavior. I practiced his approach on my friends, classmates, teachers, and even the principal of my school, and I eventually built a strong network of allies. I enjoyed an excellent reputation with my teachers and principal of the school, and my classmates and friends admired me for my genuineness and my ability get things done while treating everyone with respect and courtesy and making everyone around me feel better about themselves. Others viewed me the same way I viewed myself: as an intelligent, capable, genuine, and caring individual.

"I carried that energy throughout my high school years and into the University of Madras, where I majored in physics and minored in both mathematics and chemistry. I believe my attitude and approach with others served me well. My college experience was positive. Soon enough, it was my final semester, and I was looking for my first real job.

I was delighted to secure a job as a sales rep at a name-brand appliance company. The salary was excellent, as were the incentives for achieving sales targets. I had to control my excitement and planned to share the news with my family at dinner. My mom hugged and kissed me when she heard the news. Everyone congratulated me—except my father. He looked me straight in the eye and said, "You are good at school, Shawn, so you should go to graduate school."

"I decided to do both. I enrolled in a graduate program to study business administration while I worked full-time. Taking three evening classes each semester kept me very busy. My first semester was the hardest because I had to learn about the different functional areas, such as accounting, finance, marketing, and management, to get up to speed with my classmates, most of whom had an undergraduate business background. Through my physics and mathematics background, I'd developed analytical and problem-solving skills and was a disciplined thinker.

"Three years later, I graduated from the program with distinction—the highest level of achievement recognized by Indian universities. By that point, I was also excelling in my job as a sales rep in ways I'm not sure even I predicted. My disciplined approach to thinking through problems, my drive to succeed, and my interpersonal skills had helped me excel at my job year after year. My second and third years, I achieved more sales than any other sales rep—not just in my state, but in all of India. My first promotion came in year four, when I was promoted to area manager. Two years later, I was promoted to sales Manager and was responsible for sales throughout the state. Sales in my state was 125 percent more than in any other state."

"Wow," Darnell said quietly, raising a glass in admiration. "That's impressive, Shawn."

"Thank you," Shawn replied. "I remember those days. I would accompany my area managers and visit every major retailer and wholesaler and make a personal connection with the store owner or the general manager of the store. People always said I came across as genuine and sincere. I made a concentrated effort to understand the store's perspective, then think about how best to meet the store's needs while also achieving sales. I could read between the lines when communicating with store owners or general managers and knew when to mention promotions and discounts offered by the company to achieve sales. I became skilled at establishing a good rapport and making people comfortable, because I never pushed a sale—rather, I *wanted* them to want to buy the products.

"My consistently superior performance was noticed by the corporate office, and when the opportunity arose, I was appointed as regional sales manager and was made responsible for sales in five states. I was then reporting directly to the national sales manager. At this rate, I was on track to become the national sales manager myself sooner or later. I earned a reputation as a leader who could inspire subordinates to excel, and I lived up to this reputation by achieving the highest sales for any region in the country, even though my region was neither the most populated region nor the most prosperous region.

"Not only was my salesmanship appreciated by my company, but it was eventually noticed by other companies as well. One day, one of my closest friends, Sanjay, called me and said, 'My dad wants you to come and see him.' Pradeep, Sanjay's dad, worked as the senior architect for an engineering firm. I, of course, had met Sanjay's parents many times and knew the family well.

"After exchanging pleasantries, Pradeep went straight to the point. He said, 'Shawn, you should consider working for my firm.' I wasn't expecting such an offer and was taken off guard. My whole career, I'd worked for the same company, and things were going extremely well for me. It seemed unnecessarily risky to jeopardize my success by taking a new position, but Pradeep was determined. A week later, he took me to his company, gave me a tour of the facilities, introduced me to the general manager, who provided an overview of the company and its products and services. Pradeep mentioned that nationally there were only a dozen or so companies in the manufacturing space, and Custom Works India was among the top companies in the field. Admittedly, I was intrigued."

"Can I ask what sort of manufacturing Custom Works India was involved in?" Sarah asked, head tilted curiously.

Shawn nodded. "Yes, of course. Custom Works India worked with large manufacturers to design, build, and test prototypes of all kinds for all sorts of businesses. They also built machines for manufacturers to mass produce products—and those machines, of course, came with service contracts through Custom Works India, routing business back to us. The sales organization of Custom Works India was 350 employees strong and seemed to be doing well. The parent company, Custom Works, was a Fortune 500 company and was known for exceptional, high-quality service.

"As senior architect and longtime employee of Custom Works India, Pradeep was influential, and he arranged for me to interview with the general manager and meet other vice presidents of the company. I effortlessly connected with the other vice presidents and impressed the general manager with my knowledge of sales as well as my ability to inspire a sales organization to a higher level of productivity. I was offered the job—vice president of sales." He paused for a moment.

Everybody held their breath. "And despite the fact that I would be the vice president of sales, and that would be a huge promotion for me, I did not accept the job right away. I asked for and received two weeks to make my decision."

"Bold," said Chris with a smile, and Shawn winked at him.

"I requested access to the organization right away and expressed my desire to learn as much about the business as possible in ten days to help with my decision. It was an unusual request, which required Custom Works India to reveal aspects of their business that were kept secret from everybody except for upper-level management. I happily signed a nondisclosure agreement to gain access and assured them this was for my own edification and personal research."

"Even *more* bold," Darnell said, looking between Shawn and Chris. The group chuckled. "I don't think I've ever heard of anybody doing that before. What did you end up doing?"

"The next day," Shawn went on, "I showed up bright and early to learn the business. To break things down for a you a little bit, here's how it goes: Manufacturers with an idea for a new product will brainstorm the specifications of what that product is meant to achieve and how it would be mass produced, and then they send those to major engineering firms. Engineering firms, then, meet with the client to refine the specifications and submit a bid. If selected, the work begins, and designers are the first to start. Therefore, I first met with the designers to understand what they did and how they did it. I sat in on a few meetings with clients to see how designers elicited information from clients, sketched mock-ups of the product to scale, and revised them before handing everything over to the next group.

"Architects then designed prototypes, which engineers tested and adjusted until the product was considered effective and complete. Engineers with different backgrounds—such as mechanical, materials, metallurgy, and civil—worked together to design and develop machines to manufacture the products. Once the machines were developed and were in working order, the manufacturing department would take over production. The logistics department then worked with the client and sales organization to deliver and install the product, and the sales organization then attempted to negotiate service contracts with clients. These meetings enabled me to develop a good understanding of the internal workings of the organization.

"Now, I had to understand how the sales process worked—after all, I would be responsible for sales if I took the job. With the help of the general manager, I invited several clients, some new and some long-time clients, to a focus group meeting to find out what exactly clients look for when reviewing bids—or, in other words, why some bids were successful and some unsuccessful. The meeting was also attended by the general manager, who was curious to find this out for himself and openly wondered why he'd never thought of this idea. I learned a great deal from the focus group meeting and felt confident I could do the job; in fact, I gained a few insights I could use to boost company sales and enrich service contracts to increase revenue. However, I still was unsure if I should switch companies and take the offer.

"I had a long conversation with the person I respected the most— my dad. We both established I had an inherent talent for sales, that I was a good salesman and could be successful in any industry. Second, I had spent ten years with the same company, selling the same products to pretty much the same customers; I did not feel challenged, although achieving a sales target was always a grind. Third, I wasn't learning new skills. Fourth, the new job would bump my salary by 40 percent and my bonus by another 10 percent. I certainly could use the extra income to save even more for my kids' college education down the road. By the way, I am not married, nor do I have any kids—I'm just thinking ahead. Finally, Custom Works India was a subsidiary of Custom Works—a US-based, worldwide company with a strong reputation for high-quality, exceptional service. I decided to step out of my comfort zone and accepted the job.

"I spent the first three weeks learning more about the business. I met with other vice presidents, and with their approval, I then met with all of the company's department managers to learn what each department did and how they worked together. Many in the organization were surprised a sales guy would show so much interest in what they did and make such an effort to learn their roles. I not only learned about the inner workings of the organization but, more importantly, made important connections with key people in the organization. Through these interactions, I developed my social capital and a reputation as someone who genuinely wanted to learn about the business.

"The next two weeks were spent meeting with my sales reps to gain as much knowledge about the sales process as possible—the challenges and opportunities that lay ahead, especially. I gathered as much information as I could about the business's key competitors to discern each competitor's strengths and weaknesses. This latter process enabled me to personally connect with my sales force.

░   ░   ░

"It took me a few additional weeks to process all this information and develop a strategy. First, I created a new position, technical sales liaison, which would serve as a liaison between the sales rep and the engineers designing, building, and testing prototypes and, later, the manufacturing organization as well. The job would require a good understanding of what it took to get the finished product to the customer, as well as a strong technical background. I created this new position because I realized sales reps knew very little about the process involved in product development, and therefore they couldn't communicate effectively with the engineering staff. Second, in consultation with the other vice presidents and with the blessing of the general manager, I launched a pilot program. The pilot program consisted of organizing project teams that would include engineers with the different backgrounds needed to meet the needs of a particular client. As a team, they would work concurrently on designing, building, and testing prototypes, and the team would include a manufacturing representative to ensure smooth transition from product development to product manufacturing. And yes, each team would include a technical sales liaison.

"Eventually, it was time to run my experiment, and I had butterflies in my stomach—just like I did when standing on the line waiting for the signal to run the one-hundred-meter dash. I had quickly gained some social capital, was thought of as an intelligent person, and really wanted the experiment to succeed—not only to prove my worth as a new hire but for the sake of benefiting the company and facilitating its growth.

"At any given time, the company was working on two dozen prototypes. In consultation with the other vice presidents, I identified equivalent projects as they came in and randomly assigned one to the new work arrangement and the other to the existing work procedures. In essence, the experiment involved five projects assigned to existing work procedures and five projects to the pilot program.

"Over the next several months, the other vice presidents and I carefully monitored data related to these ten projects. For instance, we documented cost data from an accounting perspective, monitored the time it took for the product to move from one stage to the next, and measured customer satisfaction.

"When the data were collected and analyzed, the results were clear: not only were the customer satisfaction ratings higher at all measurement points in the pilot program, but the projects in the pilot program took 40 percent less time to complete and cost the company 30 percent less than projects completed through existing procedures. The vice presidents and the general manager were thrilled, as this meant huge savings for the company, and customers were extremely happy with the shorter time to market. Of course, I was overjoyed, but I was also cautious not to jump to conclusions. With the general manager's permission, I extended the experiment for another six months, because I knew the difficulty of deciding equivalence of projects and the many other factors that could have influenced the results. Fortunately, the results of the replication study were very similar to results of the first experiment. The organization embarked on a reorganization, and from that point on, the pilot program became a permanent procedure within the company.

"Custom Works India was rated number one in quality and number one in customer satisfaction a year after the reorganization and has received those scores every year since then. The CEO of Custom Works was amazed at what I had done and sent teams from all over the world, including the US, to India to learn about how Custom Works India operated. Three years later, when the general manager retired, I was appointed general manager of Custom Works India. There was no question who would be named general manager—the decision was unanimous."

John reached forward, extending his hand for Shawn to shake. "Nice work, my man." He turned to look at Chris, Jill, and Sarah.

"You guys are all too good—I'm glad I went first before you set such a precedence."

Chris shook his head, looking at Shawn. "It's like every story is better than the previous."

"You are all accomplished individuals," J Mo said. "Winners in your own right. So to compare your stories would be like comparing a figure skater to a high jumper." J Mo gestured to Shawn. "Shawn's story highlights two important concepts, reputation and political skill, which I can elaborate on, if you'd like."

Everyone in unison reached for a second drink and said, "Please do, J Mo," Jill said. Everyone nodded their heads in agreement and reached for a second drink.

UNDERLYING THEORETICAL FRAMEWORK

J Mo began by stating that two theoretical perspectives informed Shawn's journey. The first was the socioanalytic theory of personality, which provided the overarching framework influencing Shawn's personal and professional success, while the second—political skill—helped explain his natural innovativeness.

"The socioanalytic theory of personality, proposed by Robert Hogan and his colleagues, suggests that personality reflects individual motives to 'get along and get ahead,' and proposes that how we see ourselves reflects our identity. In contrast, reputation is in the eye of the beholder and is reflected in how one is perceived and described by others. Furthermore, social skill moderates this relationship—meaning that with social skill, people are more likely to establish a reputation that aligns with their self-concept and identity. Political skill is a type of social skill that enables individuals to build favorable reputations and benefit from consequences that come from having a favorable reputation.

"Let's dive into political skill with more thoroughness. According to Jerry Ferris and his colleagues, political skill is an interpersonal style variable composed of social astuteness, interpersonal influence, networking ability, and apparent sincerity. Social astuteness involves the ability to read people and situations and to understand social interactions. Interpersonal influence incorporates an adaptive, flexible orientation that permits individuals to calibrate and adjust their behavior to different contexts in ways that bring about desired responses from others. Networking ability involves the capacity to develop and leverage alliances, and apparent sincerity enables politically skilled individuals to instill trust and confidence while disguising other possible intentions.

"Now, the question is, how did Shawn develop political skill?" J Mo paused, looking at the people assembled around the fire. "Shawn developed sincerity by watching his parents interact with his grandmother, uncle, and aunt and by the way his dad related with his subordinates. They were genuine in their interactions and how they treated one another. So, being genuine and sincere came naturally to him, as everyone around him modeled those behaviors. Shawn was not only a good student who helped other students, he was also involved in several sports, such as cricket, soccer, and track. Thus, he was connected to people from different groups and enjoyed a good network of friends. Observing his dad interact with subordinates helped him improve his ability to read social situations and, ultimately, how to figure out what to say and when and how to say it so others saw him in the most favorable light. An illustration of his interpersonal influence early on was his election as class leader from fifth to eleventh grade, and then being elected as school pupil leader his senior year. His interpersonal influence enabled him to fundraise for Sunil's family when Sunil lost his dad to a car crash, as well help his mom, Sangeeta, get a job. Observing and learning from his dad helped Shawn hone his political skills from an early age, and other experiences at school enhanced his confidence in his ability to use to those skills to achieve success.

"This bled into Shawn's professional success, too, of course. He used his political skills to excel in sales and used his networking ability to connect with virtually anybody he needed to. His social astuteness acted sort of like his very own personal radar, informing him of what it would take to close a sale—be it mentioning promotions, discounts, or simply relating with the customer in a personal way in order to establish a sense of trust.

"As a sales rep, he used his interpersonal influence and social astuteness to achieve higher sales figures compared to his coworkers, and as sales manager, sales in his state were higher than sales in any other state. This confirmed that it wasn't by happenstance that he was generating such levels of success. In fact, as a regional sales manager, once again, sales in his region were substantially higher than in any other region. He was the common denominator.

"At Custom Works India, he used his social astuteness to study the internal environment and sales organization of the company to identify opportunities for improvement. He showed a genuine interest in learning and met with other vice presidents and department managers to learn about that internal environment. By showing he genuinely cared and by networking, he was able to build social capital. He then used this social capital and interpersonal influence to convince the vice presidents and the general manager to conduct an experiment putting his theories to the test. Thus, they piloted a program. To convince himself and others, he replicated the experiment, and as expected, results indicated both cost and time to market could be reduced. These results were helpful in restructuring the organization to make it more effective and efficient.

"The benefits of political skills are pretty clear. Politically skilled individuals maneuver the social context in organizations effectively and gain influence and a sense of self-confidence along the way. Political skill is a personal attribute that facilitates the success of agentic behaviors—such as proactive behaviors—in organizations. It has also been found to be related to a more favorable reputation, higher job performance ratings, and greater career progression and success, including career satisfaction. Political skill also enhances the effectiveness of influence tactics, personal initiatives, and positive personality traits, such as proactive personality and conscientiousness.

"Now, let's discuss how Shawn specifically benefitted from his political skills. Shawn achieved the role of regional sales manager within only a few short years. At Custom Works India, he was able to use his political skills, along with his other abilities, to restructure an established organization and further enhance revenue and profits, reduce time to market, and improve customer satisfaction. When the general manager retired, he was the obvious choice and was promoted to the role. Thus, Shawn's political skills helped him achieve career success and satisfaction."

How to Apply These Ideas to Achieve Success

J Mo continued, "If you want others to share your perception of how you see yourself, develop and learn how to use political skills to your advantage. First, be genuine in your interactions, so people perceive you as someone who is sincere, genuine, and caring." J Mo marked the second point by counting it on a finger. "Second, develop social astuteness—which, again, is the ability to read a situation with a heightened sense of discernment. Discernment is akin to intuition in that it contributes to one's ability to detect the hidden motivations and agendas of others. Third, network to develop social connections, as the more positive relationships you have, the better. The more networked you are, the higher your social capital. Fourth, increase your interpersonal influence by making people comfortable around you, communicating effectively, establishing a good rapport, and getting people to like you. Know that politics is a fact of organizational life. There is nothing inherently good or bad about political skills; it is how you use these skills and for what purpose that matters. Developing and effectively using political skills has many advantages and could contribute to your success in organizations, just as it did for Shawn."

In What Situations Will Implementing These Ideas Be Most Effective?

"Political skill," J Mo went on, "is a personal resource that can be used to one's advantage in any situation. Politically skilled individuals emerge as leaders in organizations. They are successful in bringing about change because they know what to say to persuade others, have a network of supporters, and appear genuine and sincere in their communications. These ingredients are necessary to persuade others to buy a product or service or to convince others a change is necessary. Just like career adaptability, political skill is also a malleable construct, which means with planning and effort, you could increase your political skill."

6

Adopting a Promotion Focus to Facilitate Career Outcomes

Day five began with a good breakfast. By then, Dana and Jean knew exactly how each person wanted their omelets. The forecast called for clear blue skies, temperatures in the mideighties, and a light breeze. With backpacks ready, the group set out for the day. They traveled in three vehicles, and after an hour, they reached their destination—another town on the Ohio river. No one in the group knew where they were going, so it was a surprise when they reached the destination. There were shops, restaurants, and cafes lined up for half a mile on one side of the river. The shops were anchored by a river boat casino on one end and a movie theater complex on the other. J Mo said, "You can walk around, eat and drink at a restaurant of your choice, and gamble if you wish—but let's meet near our parked vehicles at 4:00 p.m."

John, Darnell, and Michael went straight to the casino. Shawn and Chris went to a café and planned to go to the bookstore after coffee.

Jill, Kim, and Sarah took off shopping. They returned right on time, carrying multiple shopping bags.

"Looks like everyone had a good time," said Dana. Of course, everyone had, and they were all smiles.

Back at the lodge, everyone enjoyed a dinner consisting of grilled chicken, lasagna, carrots, beans, and roasted potatoes, with brownies and ice cream for dessert. After dinner, gathered around the firepit with a drink in hand, everyone was ready for the next story.

Kim raised her hand and said, "I will go next. But I must warn you that mine isn't as interesting as the others I've heard so far."

In response, Sarah noted, "Each of us is special in own way, so there isn't any comparison. We are all very eager to get to know you even more."

Everyone nodded.

Kim smiled at Sarah but seemed unconvinced. She paused, staring into the flames. Then she said, "Before I start, I need to let you know that my story is very much intertwined with Kathy's—and soon you'll learn about Kathy, too. By the way, I called Kathy a couple of days ago to ask her approval to share our story, and she was fine with it. She wanted me to take a group picture and send it to her. So, can we take a picture now, while there is still light?"

Everyone agreed and posed for several pictures.

"Thanks for the pictures," said Kim. "Okay, I am ready to share my story now . . .

"Kathy and I have been best friends since middle school. We started off as next-door neighbors, after her family moved from Ohio to Illinois when we were just twelve. After middle school, Kathy and I ended up going to the same high school. We both ran cross-country, belonged to the same clubs, and enjoyed going to the movies during our free time. We were inseparable—hence our nickname, K & K. Even the teachers called us K & K.

"We were good students, got straight As, and had similar vocational interests. Naturally, we both majored in business, studying accounting and finance, and—you guessed it—went to the same college, the University of Illinois at Urbana-Champaign. We grew up in Joliet, about an hour from Urbana-Champaign. We decided to room together in a freshmen dormitory.

■ ■ ■

"Kathy's parents were strict disciplinarians. She called them Drill Sergeants—DS 1 and DS 2, for short. Kathy's dad, Rudolph, was a perfectionist, and her mom, Diane, was the enforcer. She did not tolerate any mistakes, messiness, or unruly behavior. Kathy learned to be cautious and always remain vigilant. My parents were the complete opposite. My dad was a jokester and loved pranking others, and my mom was an easygoing, fun-loving, adventurous woman. Naturally, Kathy hung out at our place pretty much all the time.

"In college, Kathy was cautious when choosing electives and stayed within her comfort zone. She would complete all her assignments on time and make sure they were perfect before submission. For her, getting any grade less than an A was something to be avoided at all costs.

"Me, on the other hand, I take after my mom, and I was adventurous enough to take electives that aligned with my personal interests rather than my parents' or society's expectations. My goal at the time was to gain as much knowledge as possible and grow up to be a well-rounded person. I aspired to become a senior level manager and felt that gaining broad-based knowledge was crucial to my success.

"We were sharing funny college stories at the Christmas dinner Kathy's parents were hosting one year when my mom mentioned, 'I cannot believe you two will be graduating in May—that's just six months away.'

"The start to our final year of college was busy with both classes and job searching. Early in the fall semester, we applied to a dozen or so jobs and met with several recruiters through campus placement services. Fortunately, we had very good grades, internship experiences, held leadership roles in student organizations, and interviewed well. I got three job offers, and Kathy received four.

"Kathy accepted a job offer from Abbot Enterprises, as it seemed to fit with her personality. Abbott is a conglomerate, a strong and stable company in the insurance industry. Over its thirty-five-year history, it has not laid off any employees. Abbott pays market wages, and career paths are clearly laid out.

"I joined AMD, Inc.—a progressive company operating in a highly competitive market. AMD, Inc. is a results-oriented company, so employees who perform well are rewarded handsomely and those who fail to get results are simply let go.

"We were very happy with our job offers and eager to start working as staff accountants. Our office buildings were fifteen minutes apart—walking distance—in downtown Chicago, so we rented a two-bedroom apartment downtown.

"Kathy, as usual, was very diligent in her work. She would carefully check her work before turning it in, and her supervisor, Stacy, really appreciated her thoroughness and attention to detail. Sometimes, Kathy would stay late to help a coworker finish their project, and Stacy would vocalize how much she appreciated Kathy's willingness to help others. At the end of the year, Kathy received a very good performance review, a pay increase, and a sizeable annual bonus. The next few years went well. Kathy was happy with her life and was dating Kevin, who worked in the same building but for a different company.

"During one of their monthly meetings, Stacy asked if Kathy wanted to take on any new, different responsibilities. Kathy consulted with me. She wasn't sure if that would be a good idea, as she was very comfortable with the type of work she was currently doing. Taking on different projects would mean learning new things and perhaps making a few mistakes here and there. So, after considering the downside of working on new projects, she declined the offer. Things were going well for Kathy and her attitude was *if it ain't broke, don't fix it.*

"A couple of years went by. There was a vacancy for a manager's position at the Milwaukee office, and Kathy was invited to apply. After all, Kathy was a solid employee who excelled at her job. Working as a manager meant she would be making more and would be eligible to receive a higher percentage of her annual salary as a bonus. While she could use the extra income, she wasn't sure she really needed it. On the other hand, she would have to move an hour and half away from Kevin and nearly three hours away from her family in Joliet. In her mind, the losses outweighed the gains, and minimizing losses and ensuring security was always her priority. So, she declined the invitation to apply for the job, content with what she currently had. Soon after, Kathy and Kevin broke up, as Kathy was having second thoughts about her attraction to men. She felt more comfortable and relaxed around woman.

"I was really enjoying my job and my colleagues. My boss, Nancy, was awesome. She gave me a lot of autonomy, and I relished the freedom to do things my way. I wanted to make a difference. I would suggest ways to improve our existing policies and procedures, and Nancy, a forward-thinking manager, always appreciated my suggestions. I was committed to my work and worked hard, and I'd like to think I made a positive difference. At the end of the year, I received a great performance evaluation and a very good bonus. One of my coworkers, whose performance did not meet company standards, was let go—clearly signaling the importance of performance and contributions to the work unit.

"Work was going well. So, when Nancy asked if I wanted to take on a few new projects, I jumped at the chance. Working on a variety of projects not only increased my knowledge of the company itself but also boosted my confidence as an employee. When Nancy's husband, who worked for a different company, got transferred to the Atlanta office, Nancy decided to follow him and work from AMD's Atlanta office. Given my experience with a variety of projects and my inclination to improve work policies and procedures, I was promoted to Nancy's job. I became the manager of the unit and was responsible for the work of eight staff accountants. Our unit serviced clients from the manufacturing industry. My job was not only to supervise the eight employees but also bring in new clients from the industry.

"At first, it was rough transitioning from being an employee to supervising and managing the very same employees who were originally my friends and coworkers. I think my coworkers respected me because I was knowledgeable, had a strong work ethic, and always focused on improving things. So, over time, they accepted me as their manager. It took me a few months to get used to the new role. After that, I focused on bringing in new clients. Over the next two years, I was able to bring in seven additional clients and hired three new employees. I was enhancing my skill set and felt comfortable leading my work unit.

"By this point, Kathy and I had been roommates for a very long time. After her breakup with Kevin, she seemed rather quiet and distant, as if she was holding back something from me. One night, we went out to eat with our mutual friends. We had a few drinks and walked back to our apartment. Kathy was quiet on the way back. As soon as we entered our apartment, Kathy hugged me and kissed me on my forehead. We hug each other all the time, but this time, it felt different. I don't know what came over me; I kissed her on her lips, and Kathy kissed me back and said, 'I've been wanting to do this for a long time. I have been in the closet for so long—I can't stand it anymore.'

※　　※　　※

"We were behaving like teenagers toward their first crush. I said, 'We have been best friends since middle school, but we're more than that now.' Three months later, we were engaged. My parents were ecstatic from the very beginning, but it took a while for Kathy's parents to warm up to the idea that their daughter was a lesbian. I think their love for me helped them overcome the huge shock and accept us as a couple. We got married last year, and it was the best day of my life."

"Congratulations to you both," Sarah interjected, raising her glass of wine. Everyone in the group followed her lead, raising their drinks in a brief toast.

"Thank you," Kim said, face glowing. "Anyway, a couple of years ago, the director vacancy at AMD's office in Indianapolis caught my attention. This vacancy was in line with my aspirations and was the next logical stepping stone for me. The job meant a substantial pay increase and a bigger bonus but would involve managing three different units, each servicing clients from a different industry. The learning curve would be steep, but I was focused on what I could gain and not so much on what I would have to give up. Well, I would have to put in longer hours, learn about the different industries, and obviously move to Indy. I am adventurous, and relocating did not bother me. What I could gain weighed heavily on my mind, and after discussing it with Kathy, I decided to give it a go. Kathy assured me that she could easily transfer to Indy as well, because Abbot Enterprises had offices in every major city, and they were hiring at almost every location. I applied and interviewed for the job. I was fortunate to receive an offer, because I'd heard the competition for the position was stiff. Within a week, Kathy was able to obtain a transfer to the Indy office and would be doing the same thing she was doing in the Chicago office.

"Two months ago, we closed on a nice house in a very good neighborhood. We started moving in about three weeks ago, and Kathy is back home making sure all our stuff is put away and the house is in perfect order. She loves doing that kind of stuff. We are a happy couple and are in a good place."

Sarah said, "What a lovely story. Congratulations, again. I am happy for you guys."

"You two have known each other for a long time," Darnell added. "I hope I'm not overstepping when I say this, but . . . how did you not realize you had feelings for each other sooner?"

Kim laughed a little, waving her hand in a way that suggested she and Kathy had wondered the same thing themselves. "You're right. We had feelings for each other all along—but I think we both assumed those feelings were emanating from a place of friendship and platonic love, rather than romantic love."

Jill smiled and said, "Kim, you're really lucky to have married your best friend."

"So," Chris chimed in, "now you're both happy, have just started new jobs, bought a new house, and finished moving to a new city—I think your story is plenty exciting and impressive. You and Kathy are both successful in your own ways."

J Mo nodded. "Kathy and Kim have different orientations and approach life in different ways, but each is successful and happy. That is an important point."

"How so?" asked Shawn.

UNDERLYING THEORETICAL FRAMEWORK

"You see," J Mo began, "Kathy and Kim have different orientations. Their orientations can be understood from Tory Higgins's regulatory focus theory. Regulatory focus theory suggests that people vary in how they approach pleasure and avoid pain. Such variance is reflected by the regulatory focus, which distinguishes *promotion* focus from *prevention* focus. The theory stems from the notion that people are motivated to minimize discrepancies between actual and desired end states, or seek pleasure, and maximize the discrepancy between actual and undesired end states, or avoid pain. The orientation toward seeking pleasure is considered a promotion focus, whereas the orientation toward avoiding pain is considered a prevention focus.

"Individuals with a promotion focus are concerned with nurturance, growth, and advancement, and they pursue goals as hopes and aspirations. Promotion-focused individuals typically pursue goals using eager strategies, reflected in behaviors such as searching for new information that could help them achieve goals. They are sensitive to the presence or absence of positive outcomes, such as gains or nongains. When individuals with a promotion focus are exposed to situations that may lead to future gains, they experience a state of regulatory fit and are motivated to achieve gains. Individuals with a promotion focus are open to taking risks to reach a better state.

"In contrast, individuals with a prevention focus are concerned with safety and security and pursue goals as duties, obligations, and responsibilities. Prevention-focused individuals typically pursue goals through vigilant strategies, reflected in behaviors such as carefully vetting potential downsides and fixating on the possibility that things might go wrong. They are sensitive to failure and are focused on minimizing losses at all costs, even if it means they must forever maintain the status quo.

"Personality and early childhood experiences shaped Kathy's disposition toward prevention focus and Kim's disposition toward promotion focus. Kathy's dad was a perfectionist, which means he was focused on avoiding mistakes. Her mom was a disciplinarian and did not tolerate mistakes. Growing up in such an environment led Kathy to adopt a prevention focus. Kim, on the other hand, grew up in a more relaxed environment with a jokester dad and an easygoing, adventurous mom and consequently was focused on aspirations leading to a promotion focus."

How Adopting a Particular Focus
Shapes Career Outcomes

"Even in college, Kathy carefully avoided elective courses outside her comfort zone, minimizing her chances of failure. When it came to selecting a job offer, she preferred to work for a stable company in a conservative industry that afforded a high level of job security. She displayed her risk aversiveness first by declining to work on different projects and later by declining to apply for a promotion opportunity. She was making good money, was happy with her job and with all she had, and her goal was to maintain her status quo. Making more money or advancing in her career was not as interesting to her as maintaining the stability and security she had achieved in her current position.

◼ ◼ ◼

"In contrast, Kim took different types of elective courses to broaden her knowledge and accepted a high risk/high reward job. She voiced her opinions, made constructive suggestions for improvement, took on different projects, and when asked, took the manager position. A few years later, she applied for and received the director position. She was inspired by her aspirations, took risks, and focused on gaining *more* than what she had, rather than worrying about *losing* what she had.

"An important point, though, is that both Kathy and Kim are happy with their careers; it is just that Kim, by adopting a promotion focus, achieved a higher level of objective career success, in the form of more money, a higher bonus, and advancement.

Shawn's brows furrowed. "Is it possible to change one's focus? Is that something we have control over, or is it hardwired into our personality?"

"That's a great question," said J Mo. "First, it is important to realize people are *predisposed* to adopt either a promotion focus or a prevention focus. Having said that, is it possible to change? The answer seems to be yes. Research shows that situational cues can prime an individual to adopt one focus or the other. For instance, situational cues that emphasize nurturance needs, attainment of ideals, and potential gains tend to induce a promotion mindset, whereas situational cues that emphasize security needs, fulfillment of obligations, and potential losses tend to induce a prevention mindset. Developing the habit of systematically evaluating decision options through both the promotion frame and the prevention frame allows for a more careful consideration of those options.

"For instance, managers who engage in structuring behaviors—such as providing instructions for task completion—or who are task-focused are likely to influence their subordinates to adopt a prevention focus. Whereas those who engage in consideration behaviors—such as supporting and nurturing—are likely to influence their subordinates to adopt a promotion focus."

How to Apply These Ideas to Achieve Success

"As we grow and mature, we develop habitual ways of interacting with the environment. These characteristics are understood in terms of dispositions—such as personality, mindset, or regulatory focus. First, understand your predisposition, whether you are disposed to habitually adopt a promotion or prevention focus. Adopting each framework has consequences. Those adopting a promotion focus are motivated by gains, want to improve the status quo, and are thus willing to try new things, even if they are risky. Conversely, those with a prevention focus are motivated to avoid losses, maintain the status quo, and are very risk averse.

"Second, develop the capacity to be able to switch between these two frameworks. Evaluating decision options through the promotion framework and then evaluating those same options through the prevention framework takes effort and disciplined thinking.

"Developing such flexibility will allow you to make sound decisions likely to lead to desirable career outcomes. Third, identify what situational cues prompt you to adopt a promotion or prevention frame of mind. Becoming aware of these cues will help you make more informed choices in the future."

In What Situations Will Implementing These Ideas Be Most Effective?

"We make decisions all the time—whether they are trivial, like what to eat for breakfast, or more consequential, like accepting a job offer. We make decisions as individuals, as couples, as a family, and as members of an organization. When making consequential decisions, we need to be mindful of our predisposed orientation, because we are likely to approach the decision-making process from that perspective and be influenced by it. Developing the ability to switch one's focus is a valuable skill, as it allows you to get the best of both worlds when making decisions."

Shawn said, "Now I understand why people approach life and make decisions based on different criteria and how these criteria may lead to certain levels of career success, even though people with these orientations may be equally happy with their lives."

J Mo nodded. "You nailed it." He then turned to face the group, and with a sigh, said, "Okay, it's getting late, and we have a long day tomorrow. Let's call it a night."

Slowly, everyone headed back to their cabins—except Sarah and Shawn, who headed toward the woods.

7

Enhancing Performance through Fairness and Feedback

Day six was cloudy, with a forecasted high in the low eighties. As usual, Dana and Jean served a good breakfast everyone enjoyed. Most had already left when Shawn and Sarah arrived for breakfast. They sat together and were involved in an animated conversation.

By nine o'clock, the backpacks were ready, and everyone started arriving at the sitting room, ready to go. J Mo showed up right at 9:30 and asked if everyone was ready. After a resounding yes, he led the way.

The group hiked for nearly two hours to a huge lake, ate their lunch, and rested for thirty minutes. After that, they walked to a cove lined with tall trees and overgrown shrubs, where they started fishing.

Sarah commented, "Fishing is very relaxing for me."

"Yes, and it's so fun when you end up catching a lot of fish," Darnell added. And sure enough, they caught a lot of fish. In two hours, they caught twenty-one fish—eight of which were over five pounds each.

In all, it was a good fishing trip. At two o'clock that afternoon, they decided to pack up their fishing gear and head back to the lodge. Jill said, "With all this walking and eating healthy—instead of my usual lounging in front of the TV with takeout—I feel like I've lost a lot of weight."

"Me too!" echoed John.

"The first thing I'm going to do when I get back is weigh myself," said Michael. "I bet I've lost seven to ten pounds by now."

Dana and Jean quickly processed some of the fish the group had caught and prepared it for dinner. "Nothing like eating fish that was caught just a few hours ago," said Jean. After a hearty meal of fish, rice, steamed vegetables, and dessert, half the group went for a stroll, while the others went back to their cabins to refresh. By eight o'clock that evening, everyone had gathered around the firepit, ready to hear the next story.

Darnell raised his hand and said, "Only Michael and I are left. And if Michael doesn't mind, I'd like to go next."

Michael nodded and said, "Go right ahead, my friend."

Darnell started by saying, "I'm privileged to be a part of this group, and I'm thankful for J Mo's insightful analyses. I have learned a lot about each of you from your stories, and I hope you learn as much about me from my story. I grew up in the West End neighborhood of Atlanta and was practically raised by my grandmother, as my dad traveled quite a bit for his construction job. I don't know if you know this, but the West End is one of the poorest neighborhoods in Atlanta. My younger sister and I were very close—still are—and she is only three years younger than me. Growing up, we had many mutual friends, and we played basketball all the time, at home and in high school. Grandma instilled the importance of work ethic and emphasized the value of getting a good education. She would often say, 'Get a good education, get a good job, and take me with you to the north side, maybe Buckhead.'

"Grandma's words stuck in my head. I did well in school. Growing up in West End, I saw inequities all around me, and I saw how such inequities shaped people's attitudes and behaviors. When people were treated badly by others, they did bad things to get revenge, which only led to a downward spiral. It was a vicious cycle, and people could not seem to break out of it. This observation led me to develop a deep sense of fairness; I wanted to treat others with fairness, just as I wanted others to treat me fairly.

"I was the first to go to college in my family. I majored in psychology with a focus in industrial and organizational psychology. My first job was working as an HR recruiter for a major job boards company. At the beginning, the job was interesting, and I was very excited, but as time passed, the job became less and less interesting. So, one day, I quit my job and decided to pursue an MBA degree. My 3.8 undergraduate GPA, 720 GMAT score, and work experience enabled me to get into the MBA program of an elite private university. I was thrilled. I decided to specialize in marketing, as I was interested in integrated marketing communications. When I'd worked as a recruiter, I had seen so many postings for experts in IMC from major marketing and advertising firms, so I knew there was a demand for that knowledge.

"I picked up valuable skills while working toward my MBA. Three months before graduation, I was hired by one of the leading marketing firms in Atlanta—Sheridan Communications, Inc. As a marketing specialist, I would be involved in developing, executing, and tracking marketing campaigns for client businesses and organizations. My job would also expose me to conducting audience research, writing campaign copy, buying media, crafting the look and feel of a display advertisement, and seeing the entire end-to-end spectrum of setting up effective marketing campaigns. I was particularly excited to use data gathering and analytics technology to evaluate the impact of marketing initiatives on consumer behavior and the perception of clients' brands so I could make appropriate recommendations to adjust clients' strategies accordingly. Twelve other marketing specialists and I reported to an assistant marketing director. Seven assistant marketing directors reported to the marketing director, who in turn reported to the VP of sales and marketing.

"I enjoyed working and living in the Buckhead area. My grandma loved the neighborhood and wanted me to save as much money as possible so we could buy a small house. My grandma was happy, which made me happier.

"I worked long hours and was committed to my job. I wasn't shy about asking questions or making mistakes, as my goal was to master the craft. Alicia, my manager, appreciated my work ethic and genuine interest in learning, and consequently, she was very generous with her time and was a true mentor.

"However, not everyone liked Alicia, as she had a temper and was known to fly off the handle at the simplest mistake, which made the work environment tense at times. While the marketing specialists experienced some slower times, work was usually fast-paced and hectic, as clients were demanding and there were deadlines to meet. Sometimes you could spend hours on a task with no results. While that was simply the nature of the job, it was a frustrating experience.

"A while after I started, it was time for annual performance evaluations, and the atmosphere in the office was noticeably tense. Neither the marketing specialists nor Alicia liked this period, as no one was happy with the evaluation process or their evaluations. Fortunately, I received a positive evaluation, but I felt the performance feedback was vague and therefore not particularly useful.

"Three of my closest colleagues received evaluations that were lower than what they had expected—which, of course, made them angry. One of them, Pat, confided that Alicia had no useful information to share with her and couldn't convincingly justify the evaluations she had given her. Pat said she was planning to quit and had started looking for a job with other marketing agencies in the Atlanta area.

"I was troubled after hearing this information, but things were going well for me at Sheridan Communications, and my boss liked me. For four years, I got good evaluations and good raises, and my salary was increased once to reflect the market rate in the Atlanta area. To add to all that, when Alicia left to become director of marketing at another agency, I was a serious contender for her position.

"My interview with the marketing director went well, as did the interview with the three assistant managers. A week later, I was offered the job. The promotion came with a nice salary bump, and I would be eligible for a bonus based on the company's profits. I had been saving money all these years, and with the salary bump, I felt comfortable with putting a down payment on a three-bedroom house. No one was happier than Grandma. My sister, Jamia, who works as a registered nurse, came to live with us, so she could save enough money to buy her own home in a few years.

"I spent the first three weeks in my new position learning about the different projects my team of marketing specialists were working on. Although, I knew my colleagues well, I was now their supervisor, and I was mindful of this new role—much like Kim was when she moved into a managerial role and had to supervise her former coworkers. Fortunately, I knew everyone's strengths and special talents, and I tried to allocate projects in such a way as to maximize team performance.

"I instituted weekly meetings with my subordinates, during which I expected them to give me updates on their work, including reports on the resources they needed and the constraints they faced. Systematically collecting this information allowed me to develop a good sense of each person's effort level, the results achieved, and the constraints and challenges associated with their work. I was genuinely interested in my employees and did everything I could to make them productive, make their work easier, and create an engaged work environment.

"I was collecting information through weekly meetings for the sole purpose of staying on top of things, but this information proved to be very useful in evaluating performance of my employees. Before assigning performance ratings, I deeply considered every aspect of the employee's success or lack thereof—including their effort level, the resources they were provided, and any potential constraints standing in the way of their success. Second, I identified two strengths and two areas of improvement for each employee. Armed with this information, I scheduled one-on-one meetings with each employee and delivered feedback. Ten of the thirteen marketing specialists indicated they felt their performance was evaluated fairly—which, again, has been a priority of mine from the start. Only three employees pointed out additional information I should have considered but had missed. I took their feedback into consideration and, upon reflection, did the right thing—revised my evaluations to the satisfaction of the three employees.

███

"Out of curiosity, I looked at the company's performance appraisal form and realized the form had been created ten years ago. The marketing specialist position had evolved drastically in the last ten years, and yet the form hadn't been updated. Consequently, it included tasks that were no longer performed and omitted tasks that were currently performed by the specialists.

"In performance appraisal terminology, the criteria were contaminated and deficient. I made a mental note to take up the matter with my supervisor, the marketing director, as well as with the human resources associate assigned to the marketing area.

"With the blessing of both the marketing director and the HR department, I put together a task force consisting of three marketing specialists to revise the performance appraisal form to accurately capture the current tasks and responsibilities of a marketing specialist. In addition, given that there was also some variation between the work performed by marketing specialists, they left space on the form to enter criteria relevant to the actual work done by each specialist. In this way, the form was standardized but adaptable. In addition to revising the form, I asked the task force to codify how and what data would be collected, how employees could provide feedback on their evaluations, how the form was to be used, and how any disagreements were to be handled. I felt creating such a document was important to ensuring the procedures used to evaluate performance were fair to those whose performance was being evaluated. The task force sought input from all the marketing specialists to revise the performance appraisal form, as well as create the procedures document. It took the task force several meetings spread over the course of three months to complete the task.

"The following year, I carefully followed the procedures document to gather performance data, and just like before, carefully considered each employee's effort level and results achieved based on their full achievement potential, considering the resources made available to them. As always, I also considered any constraints the employee might have faced before determining my performance rating. During the one-on-one feedback session, I treated each subordinate with respect, dignity, and courtesy. In addition, I was candid in my communication of strengths and areas of improvement, tailored my communication to the specific needs of each employee, gave employees ample opportunity to participate in the discussion, and offered constructive and useful suggestions to further improve performance and contributions.

"Most everyone felt that their performance evaluations accurately reflected their actual performance and contributions, that procedures were followed, that the feedback was candid and clear, and that they were treated in a respectable manner during the entire process. In short, they were satisfied with the performance appraisal process and the feedback they received.

"As you know, fairness is very important to me, and I was glad all the work we put in seemed to be paying off. Performance of many of my subordinates improved, and satisfaction scores from clients also showed a noticeable improvement. Many specialists went above and beyond their prescribed job duties to contribute to the unit by helping each other, suggesting improvements, and engaging in various types of prosocial behaviors. The work environment improved, and specialists eagerly sought feedback from me and from each other in the effort of continuously enhancing their performance.

"My employees are productive, are happy, and go above and beyond to help one another and to provide excellent service to our clients. I love my job and the work environment. And that is my story," Darnell finished.

Jill said, "Yes, fairness is very important to me as well."

"I've learned that when you treat people fairly, they will also treat you fairly," noted Chris.

J Mo nodded and added, "Managers need to work hard to create a fair workplace, and that is exactly what Darnell succeeded in doing."

"Please elaborate, J Mo," said John, and the others nodded their heads in agreement.

UNDERLYING THEORETICAL FRAMEWORK

J Mo began by saying, "The construct of fairness, or justice, has been broadened in recent years, so let's trace its evolution back to the root to best understand what it is and how it applies to the workplace.

"In the 1960s, John Stacey Adams proposed what is called *equity theory*—which is now referred to as *distributive justice.* Distributive justice deals with the fairness of the allocation of outcomes, stating that outcomes—performance evaluations, pay raises, bonuses—should be proportional to inputs—education, knowledge, skill, effort, results achieved, and so forth. A person will perceive distributive justice when he or she feels the outcome they receive is proportional to their contribution and that this ratio equals that of others. Thus, if John received a 4 percent raise and Peter a 5 percent raise, and John feels that Peter contributed more and deserves the 5 percent raise relative to his 4 percent raise, John will perceive distributive justice; that is, the pay increase he received relative to what John received to be fair.

"A second fairness concept, *procedural justice*—introduced by John Thibaut and Laurens Walker—deals with the fairness of procedures used to allocate outcomes. Research shows that procedural justice is just as important as distributive justice, if not more so. Fair procedures ensure that outcomes will be fair in the long run. On the other hand, if procedures are deemed unfair, the likelihood of receiving unfair outcomes in the future increases, diminishing hope for the future.

"So, what is the definition of fair? What constitutes a fair procedure? The concept of procedural justice suggests that procedures are only fair when they encompass the following attributes: First, employees must be given the opportunity to provide feedback on the procedure itself, and their feedback must be considered by upper management. Second, the procedure must be free from bias, based on accurate information, and applied consistently. And last but not least, the procedure must be based on moral and ethical standards. It is also highly important that employees are given the opportunity to appeal the outcomes that result from these procedures.

* * *

"Robert Bies and Joseph Moag extended justice theory by introducing a third justice concept—interactional justice. Interactional justice has two components: interpersonal justice and informational justice.

"Interpersonal justice deals with the fairness of treatment—that is, the extent to which your supervisor treats you with dignity, respect, and common courtesy. Informational justice deals with the fairness of information sharing—that is, when confronted or questioned, the extent to which your supervisor provides information in a candid manner, tailors his communication to meet your specific needs, provides clear explanations for his actions that impact you, and communicates with you in a timely manner, so the explanations are clear and the information useful."

How Did Darnell Develop a Sense of Justice or Fairness?

"Growing up in the West End neighborhood, Darnell was surrounded by poverty and all the inequities typically associated with poverty, such as lack of opportunity to receive a good education or a stable home environment. The latter, especially, will lead people to engage in unproductive behaviors, such as loitering, stealing, getting into fights, and so forth, which further exacerbate the problems associated with poverty. The awareness of the dysfunctional consequences of inequity prevented him from falling into the vicious downward spiral. He developed a strong sense of justice, and it became one of his core values."

How Did Darnell Apply Justice Concepts to Ensure Fairness?

"When Darnell was promoted to the assistant manager position and the time came to evaluate the performance of his employees, his overriding concern was evaluating their performance in a fair manner and that his evaluations accurately reflected the contribution of each employee. During his weekly meetings with his employees, he collected information about the projects they were working on, the results they achieved, and the opportunities and constraints they faced, so he could stay on top of things. This information allowed him to have a good sense of what each employee was reasonably capable of achieving—given the constraints and obstacles they either faced or didn't face. In a few instances, when employees shared additional accomplishments, he gladly revised his evaluations so they accurately reflected performance. These actions enabled Darnell to ensure distributive justice.

"Darnell then realized the performance appraisal form was deficient and contaminated, meaning an evaluation would be based on irrelevant criteria that had nothing to do with employee performance. Therefore, he put together a task force to revise and update the form and, in addition, create a document that codified what data were to be collected, how the form was to be used, and how any disagreements would be resolved. Creating such a transparent process ensured procedural fairness, as long as those procedures were applied in a consistent manner, which he was committed to doing.

"When providing performance feedback, Darnell was sure to treat his employees fairly by being respectful and treating them with dignity. He provided feedback in a candid manner, tailored his communication to their specific needs, offered explanations to justify the evaluations provided, and offered useful and constructive feedback to help improve performance. Thus, he ensured interactional justice."

What Are the Consequences of Fairness Perceptions?

"When employees perceive outcomes are allotted fairly, fair procedures are used to allocate those outcomes, and they are treated fairly, they experience positive emotions and high levels of satisfaction with the process. Social exchange theory, by Peter Blau, suggests that exchanges, positive and negative alike, are reciprocated in kind. That is, when a manager treats employees in a fair manner, they want to give back, and they do so by engaging in prosocial behaviors, such as helping a co-worker, the supervisor, or the organization itself. Research shows that fairness enhances satisfaction and commitment and elicits citizenship behaviors from employees.

"People often mistakenly believe providing feedback *always* improves performance. In a large-scale study, Angelo DeNisi and Avraham Kluger reported that although feedback improves performance, in nearly a third of the studies, feedback *decreased* performance. Recent research shows that provision of feedback does not always result in performance improvement; rather how ratees react to performance feedback influences subsequent performance. For instance, research by

I.M. Jawahar suggests that feedback only improves performance when the recipients of feedback perceive it to be fair and are satisfied with the feedback. Thus, ensuring the fairness of performance evaluations and performance feedback is even more important, as the employees' interpretation of them will influence their future behavior."

How to Apply These Ideas to Achieve Success

"Performance management is critical to the success of any unit. Thus, managers must strive to build a performance-oriented culture. You can do that by ensuring procedural fairness of the performance appraisal process, assigning performance ratings that accurately reflect employees' contributions, treating employees with respect and dignity, communicating performance-related information in a candid and clear manner, and offering constructive suggestions for performance improvement. While organizational policies may constrain you from enhancing procedural fairness—organizations often outline processes that need to be followed, so you may not be able to change the process—the ability to ensure distributive fairness and interactional fairness is entirely within your control, and recent studies indicate that interactional justice perceptions have more impact on outcomes than either distributive or procedural justice."

In What Situations Will Implementing These Ideas Be Most Effective?

"If you supervise employees, you will be required to evaluate the performance of those employees and allocate pay increases. Research shows that employees dread receiving performance appraisals just as much as supervisors dread evaluating performance and giving feedback. This challenge is exacerbated because every employee believes himself or herself as an above average or even a superior performer, which is termed as the Lake Wobegon Effect. It is named for the fictional town of Lake Wobegon from the radio series *A Prairie Home Companion*, where, according to Garrison Keillor, 'all the children are above average.' In a similar way, a large majority of people claim to be above average; this phenomenon has been observed among drivers, CEOs, stock market analysts, college students, and state education officials, among others.

"If you are already in a supervisory position, take time to evaluate the performance appraisal process. If you were recently promoted to a supervisory position, this is the ideal time to examine, modify, and refine the performance appraisal process."

◼   ◼   ◼

Shawn said, "Until now, I could tell you whether I thought something was fair or not, but I couldn't really describe the *why* behind it."

"Yes," said Chris thoughtfully. "Thanks to J Mo, I now understand the foundation of fairness and how it applies to performance evaluations in the workplace."

Darnell thanked J Mo by saying, "I recall reading these theories as an undergrad psychology major but had completely forgotten them. I did what I thought was the right thing to do, and it turned out well."

J Mo added, "When people perceive they are being treated fairly, they work harder, are more satisfied with their jobs, are committed to the organization, engage in citizenship behaviors, and refrain from dysfunctional or counterproductive behaviors. You can expect the opposite outcomes if people perceive unfairness."

"Absolutely," said Jill.

"Well, today we hiked for almost six hours, and it has been a long day." J Mo stood up from his seat and waved everybody toward their rooms. "I will see you all tomorrow."

CHAPTER

8

Enhancing Psychological Well-Being by Balancing Job Demands and Resources

Day seven, the last full day of the weeklong camp, was a beautiful day, with clear blue skies and highs forecasted in the low eighties. Jean added waffles to the usual breakfast. Everyone seemed excited, talking and laughing boisterously as they enjoyed their breakfast. Shawn and Sarah sat at a separate table and were once again having an animated conversation.

By 9:00 a.m., breakfast had been wrapped up and several people went to their rooms to refresh. Others simply hung around in the sitting room. J Mo arrived a few minutes before 9:30 a.m. and told everybody to be sure to bring a change of clothes, as they were likely to get wet. "Today, we'll stop at a waterfall, and some of you may decide to go for a swim," he said, much to the delight of everybody assembled. Everyone rushed to their rooms to get some spare clothes, stuffed them in their backpacks, and set out to explore.

As advertised, the group hiked for an hour to a nearby waterfall. Some stood under the falls, and others horsed around. Others swam in the waterhole created by the falling water, which fed into a robust but narrow stream. The water was crystal clear and a bit cold, although it only took a few minutes to get used to the temperature. "This is so much fun!" said Jill. Several others agreed. Darnell, Shawn, and Michael, who were standing right under the waterfall, could not hear a thing.

It was getting close to noon, and everyone was getting hungry. J Mo said, "There is a perfect spot over there for us to enjoy our lunch."

Michael asked, "Can we spend another hour in the water after we eat?" Several insisted that it was a good idea, so back they went in the water after lunch. By 2:00 p.m., they got into canoes and went downstream for about three miles, which took them nearly two hours. In many places along the way, the stream was shallow. In some places, it was necessary to literally pick up the canoe, walk a few steps, and then put it back in the water.

"This is so much fun. Why didn't we come here more often, J Mo?" asked Chris.

J Mo replied, "I was saving the best for the last day."

When they reached their destination, they pulled the canoes on the shore, placed them side by side, and began their hike back to the lodge.

Dana and Jean had prepared grilled chicken and baked fish for dinner, along with an assortment of fixings. J Mo, after consulting with Chris, the wine connoisseur, opened several bottles of wine. Everyone thanked Dana and Jean for the sumptuous dinner, and the conversation kept getting louder and louder; clearly everyone was having a good time. Although Michael was unusually quiet.

"Michael, you seem anxious," said Shawn.

Michael replied, "I'm just thinking through my story in my head, that's all."

Shawn assured him that he would be fine.

By 8:30 p.m., everyone had gathered around the firepit, and the fire was roaring.

Michael, who was still visibly nervous, asked, "Can I begin? I want to tell my story and get it over with so I can relax and enjoy this glorious night."

Everyone laughed, and Kim said, "Please begin, Michael."

⬛   ⬛   ⬛

"As many of you know by now, I am a licensed therapist dedicated to helping others. I worked as a therapist for nearly two dozen years, and six years ago, I started to take on management roles. I was managing a family-run psychological services company in Tulsa, Oklahoma. The company was founded by a man named John Fernandez, and it flourished under his leadership. He was a workaholic and never took care of himself, and one Sunday evening, he died of a massive heart attack. He was only sixty-one years old. After his sudden demise, I thought the family would sell the practice, but instead, John's son, Henry, took over the company. Henry was an accountant and knew nothing about psychological services, and working for Henry proved to be a nightmare; decisions were not always made with the best interests of patients in mind, and I found it difficult to work in such an environment. One day, I just couldn't take it anymore, so I simply quit.

"I was unemployed for three months, and I was beginning to feel worried. After applying to and interviewing for several jobs, finally I got a job as the director of the Tulsa office of Providence Services, Inc., a nationally recognized provider of mental health and behavioral services. Providence has offices in almost every major city in the US. In fact, it has multiple offices in major metropolitan areas like New York, Boston, Chicago, Atlanta, Dallas, Houston, Phoenix, Los Angeles, and a few others."

"Can I ask how large those offices are?" Chris asked.

Michael nodded. "The Tulsa office has a staff of one hundred twenty employees—eighty therapists, nine managers, two IT personnel, and twenty-nine office employees, who take care of appointments, billing, and all that.

"Within a week of starting my new job, I could sense the high stress level among fellow employees—it was palpable. The therapists were stressed, as were some of the managers. The hectic pace of the work environment along with the increasing demand for services contributed to the chaos and added to the stress level of the already stressed employees. In fact, every week, 5 to 10 percent of the therapists were calling in sick. And eight therapists had quit in the last six months. I felt as if I had quit one bad workplace only to join another.

"Realizing employees who were close to experiencing burnout would not be able to effectively help clients, I decided to change the work environment and reduce the stress level. I decided the best way to systematically gather information from employees was to conduct an anonymous survey. I put together a survey in Qualtrics and measured a variety of stressors, including role overload, role ambiguity, role conflict, time pressure, unpredictability of workload, lack of autonomy, lack of support, and lack of incentives or rewards, and poor management. To increase participation, I limited collecting demographic information to just sex and years spent in present role, promising employees I would only look at data by one demographic variable at a time, so the identity of survey respondents would remain anonymous.

"With a lot of encouragement, I received completed surveys from one hundred ten employees. An analysis of the data indicated *very* high levels of multiple stressors, not surprisingly. To gain further insight, I conducted five focus group meetings—three with therapists, one with the managers, and one with the office and clerical staff. Through these meetings, I gained additional insights and came to the realization that the most stressed group was the therapist group.

◼   ◼   ◼

"So, what was stressing the therapists out the most?" Michael asked rhetorically, and everybody in the group leaned in, as though ready to hear a secret. "The therapists could not predict their workload. It was as simple as that. They were overworked—meaning they experienced role overload—and felt they had little autonomy in terms of the clients they took on. Additionally, they did not feel supported or rewarded for their contributions. They were all salaried employees, with almost all of them working more than forty hours per week, and some even fifty hours, without any additional compensation. Furthermore, half of the employees indicated low levels of job satisfaction, and nearly a quarter expressed a strong desire to quit."

"Wow," said Jill, eyes wide. "A quarter of them were interested in quitting?"

Michael nodded grimly. "I decided to make some big changes. I didn't want to appear as an autocratic leader, so even though I had some ideas about what to do, I put together a task force, consisting of five therapists and two managers. I met with the task force and charged them with developing solutions that would lower the stress levels of the therapists. I told them I would be attending the meetings in an advisory capacity and my role would be to make sure the solutions developed were, in fact, feasible to implement and would be effective. Over a period of two months, the task force studied the problem and worked on developing recommendations. I was delighted with the task force's recommendations.

"Working closely with the managers, I instituted the following changes: First, we tackled how work was assigned. Managers were assigning clients to therapists without consulting the therapists themselves. We changed this practice. Managers were now required to present therapists with a list of clients, and the therapist could pick their next client. This new practice would ensure there was a good fit between the therapist's expertise and the needs of the client, as well as give the therapists a sense of control. This also made work—or, more precisely, their future workload—more predictable.

"Second, we created a workload policy. Records revealed some therapists worked more than fifty hours a week, while others routinely worked more than forty hours. Working that many hours, week after week, in an already stressful job will increase the likelihood of experiencing burnout. Not to mention, it strongly jeopardizes work-life balance.

"I put an end to this practice by instituting a policy that only under extraordinary circumstances could therapists work more than forty hours, and to do so, they had to obtain prior permission. This policy meant therapists had to work closely with managers on client selection to stay within the forty-hour requirement.

"Third, I calculated billable hours per therapist. It was 15 percent higher than the average across the company. I also shared with upper management the fact that seven therapists had recently quit Providence, and the results of the survey indicated very low levels of job satisfaction and high levels of turnover intentions—a known precursor to actual turnover. I used this information to receive authorization to hire seven new therapists, and I felt this addition would help reduce the workload of all therapists over time.

"Fourth, working with the managers, I created a new work procedure. Whenever a therapist took on a new client, he or she would have to start a client progress report. This report would list the client's existing ailment or diagnosis, the goal to be achieved through therapy, and the estimated time commitment. After each meeting with the client, the therapist was required to update the report and share it with their manager. This new procedure was instrumental in reducing role ambiguity, meaning the therapist clearly understood the goal each client was striving toward, and it also helped the managers estimate the time commitment of each therapist.

"Fifth, when therapists had to work more than forty hours per week to meet the needs of their clients, the additional hours were documented, and they were encouraged to compensate for the additional hours worked by taking commensurate time off in a future week.

"Sixth, we hired a consultant to conduct a series of workshops for the managers. Our managers were introduced to best management practices with respect to supporting, mentoring, coaching, and providing feedback to employees. Therapists were also encouraged to attend workshops to hone their skills. I instituted a forty-hour-per-year employee development requirement, which could be met by attending conferences, workshops, training programs, or webinars.

"It took us almost a year to fully implement these changes. Six months after implementation, I readministered the same survey. Results were remarkably different: employees, particularly the therapists, reported lower levels of role overload, less role ambiguity, reduced time pressure, more autonomy, and more support from their managers. Collectively, these indicators signaled significant reduction in job stress. Employees expressed higher levels of job satisfaction and reported lower intentions to quit. One of the longtime clerical employees specifically told me, and I quote, 'This is a totally different place than it was two years ago.' Others echoed that sentiment. Even a casual observer would be able to notice the relaxed work atmosphere, happy smiles, and sense of contentment among employees. So, I am extremely happy with the results. And that concludes my story." Michael looked quite relieved to be finished talking.

Chris commented, "Stress levels are through the roof in corporate America, and high levels of stress have negative consequences."

Everyone nodded.

J Mo added, "Making changes to reduce stress levels of employees is a remarkable achievement, so kudos to you, Michael."

Kim turned to J Mo and said, "J Mo, we can't wait for your analysis of the situation and what we can learn from it."

UNDERLYING THEORETICAL FRAMEWORK

J Mo began by saying, "A useful theory that will help you understand what Michael and his colleagues accomplished is called the job demands-resources, or JD-R, model. The JD-R model was proposed by Evangelia Demerouti, Arnold Bakker, Friedhelm Nachreiner, and Wilmar Schaufeli. This popular model proposes that all work characteristics can be categorized as either a job *demand* or a job *resource*.

"Job demands are defined as the physical, psychological, social, or organizational aspects of a job that require sustained physical or psychological effort and are therefore associated with certain physiological or psychological costs. Examples of job demands include high work pressure and emotionally demanding interactions with clients or customers.

"Job resources, on the other hand, refer to the physical, psychological, social, or organizational aspects of the job that are functional in achieving work goals, reducing job demands and the associated physiological and psychological costs, or stimulating personal growth, learning, and development. Examples of job resources are autonomy, skill variety, performance feedback, and opportunities for growth.

"Job demands and job resources instigate two very different processes, namely a health-impairment process and a motivational process.

Specifically, job demands instigate the heath-impairment process, and through it, adversely affect psychological well-being and, over time, could lead to burnout. Job resources, on the other hand, instigate a motivational process, and through it, could increase work engagement, leading to positive consequences such as higher levels of satisfaction and job performance. In addition, job resources can buffer the effects of job demands on strain, such that when resources are high, the negative influence of job demands on psychological well-being is reduced.

"Indeed, research has shown that job resources, such as autonomy, social support, performance feedback, and opportunities for professional development buffer the relationship between job demands, such as emotional demands, client harassment, workload and physical demands, and burnout. Thus, employees with more resources cope better with job demands and are less likely to experience strain or stress.

"Another model, the challenge-hindrance stress model, advanced by Marcie Cavanaugh and her colleagues, further classifies job demands as *challenge demands* and *hindrance demands*. Challenge demands are defined as job demands that require effort but that potentially promote the employee's growth and achievement. Examples of challenge stressors are high levels of workload, time pressure, and increased responsibility. Hindrance demands are defined as job demands or work circumstances that involve excessive or undesirable constraints that interfere with or inhibit an individual's ability to achieve valued goals. Examples of hindrance demands include role conflict, role overload, and role ambiguity. Hindrance demands have a more negative effect on psychological well-being and cause more strain than challenge demands.

"It is important to point out that whether a stressor is perceived as a challenge or a hindrance stressor depends on the individual, and a challenge stressor could, over time, be perceived as a hindrance stressor and vice versa."

Why Did the Therapists at the Tulsa Office Experience Strain?

"The therapists at the Tulsa office were clearly experiencing strain, as evidenced by the turnover rate and absence rate. The therapists were overwhelmed by job demands, such as working long hours due to heavy workload, unpredictability of future workload, lack of clear goals, and a lack of support. The imbalance created by high levels of job demands and low levels of job resources led the therapists to experience a high level of strain.

"Now, what are the consequences of strain, specifically? A sustained high level of strain leads to several negative *behavioral consequences*, such as increased smoking or alcohol and drug abuse, accident proneness, appetite disorders, and more. There are also *psychological consequences*, such as family or interpersonal problems, disturbed sleep, depression, and burnout. The cherry on top are the inevitable *medical consequences*, such as headaches, backaches, skin disease, heart disease, and more.

※　※　※

"Due to the above points, there are also *direct costs* to the organization as the result of reduced participation—so, tardiness, absenteeism, and a decrease in work performance. There are also *indirect costs* associated with loss of vitality—so, things like low morale, low motivation, low satisfaction, communication breakdowns, faulty or poor decision-making, deterioration of work relations, and forgone opportunity costs."

What Did Michael Do to Reduce the Stress Level?

"To reduce the stress levels experienced by the therapists, Michael rectified the job demands-resources imbalance by doing two things: reducing job demands and increasing job resources.

"First and foremost, Michael reduced job demands by hiring more therapists. By spreading work across many therapists, there was less for each to do on an individual level, thus reducing the chances of work overload and burnout. Second, he instituted the forty-hour workweek policy, thereby preventing therapists from working more than forty hours a week. This also had the benefit of helping therapists forecast their future workload. The inability to accurately forecast future workload was a hindrance stressor, which Michael was able to eliminate. Third, he reduced role ambiguity by requiring therapists to complete the client progress report, which has the purpose of clearly documenting the goal for each client and the timeline for the therapy to be completed.

"Simultaneously, Michael increased job resources. First, he increased autonomy, allowing therapists to be in control of their client base and workload. For instance, they could select their clients in consultation with their managers. Additionally, requiring therapists to work no more than forty hours a week means therapists will have time to recuperate, which is important, as replenishing energy is key to good health. Third, by training managers in best practices related to coaching, mentoring, and providing feedback, managers will be able to provide better support to therapists—which is an important job resource. Finally, Michael provided the therapists with the opportunity to develop their own skill set, thus affording them opportunities to grow and develop professionally. Collectively, these resources helped the therapists to better cope with the already greatly reduced job demands, leading to reduced stress and higher levels of psychological well-being.

"What Michael did—reducing job demands and increasing job resources—aligns nicely with the force field analysis, a concept advocated by a famous social psychologist, Kurt Lewin. Lewin said that in order to bring about change—in this case, reducing stress levels—one has to do two things: increase driving forces and reduce restraining forces. In this case, job demands were the restraining forces, and job resources were the driving forces. So, Michael increased driving forces and reduced restraining forces, thereby lowering stress levels of employees."

How to Apply These Ideas to Achieve Success

"Employee stress levels are rising nationally. Experiencing a high level of stress over extended periods of time leads to burnout, wherein employees feel physically and emotionally exhausted, become cynical, and have a diminished sense of accomplishment. Stress and burnout not only have a negative effect on the employee but also on the organization. Therefore, managers should realize individual health and organizational health are interrelated.

⬛ ⬛ ⬛

"Managers can use the job demands-resources model to analyze the work environment. The first thing to do is to discern the major job demands employees are facing. Second, in consultation with employees, classify the demands as *challenge job demands* or *hindrance job demands* and do everything possible to reduce *hindrance demands*. Second, increase job resources. When it comes to job resources, think broadly. For instance, there may be resources that could be provided by the organization—such as hiring more employees, as was the case for Michael at Providence. Think about how the supervisor could help. For instance, the supervisor could provide more support to employees, and supervisory support is an important resource. Other resources a supervisor could provide include reallocating workload, being sensitive to personal challenges an employee might be facing, offering more autonomy to employees, and providing additional resources to buffer the effect of increased workload. A manager can help increase personal resources of the employee as well, such as by sending employees to attend training and development workshops to increase their skill levels. Generally speaking, all of these are job resources, and increasing resources while simultaneously attempting to reduce job demands will help your employees maintain functional stress levels, enhance their psychological well-being, and benefit the organization through enhanced performance and contributions."

In What Situations Will Implementing These Ideas Be Most Effective?

"Demands on employees are rising for a multitude of reasons," J Mo went on. "A big reason has to do with the expectation of 24/7 connectedness in the workforce, which has been made possible by technological advancements over the last decade. Additionally, organizations want employees to do more with less.

"As an employee, you may experience work stress. If you experience work stress, you can apply the principles of the job demands-resources model to reduce stress to a manageable level. Of course, as a supervisor, you can apply these same principles to help your employees manage their stress levels.

"Managing stress is critically important, as prolonged exposure to stress has many negative consequences—most of which we've already covered. In addition, people experiencing stress are more likely to make poor decisions and have difficulty communicating and getting along with others—all of which negatively affect the organization itself."

J Mo turned to Michael, who was sitting next to him, and clapped him on the back. "Brilliant job, Michael. You've done a lot of good work."

Everyone applauded Michael's story and J Mo's expert analysis and insights.

CONCLUSION

J Mo said, "I would like to offer a few parting words. As illustrated by your stories, success means different things to different people. Success can be getting a job when you don't have one, getting a huge bonus or a promotion, or just being fully engaged in one's work. It could also mean reducing stress, increasing psychological well-being, or feeling a sense of contentment.

A second point I would like to make is this: how we define success changes with time—meaning as we progress in our careers, how we define success could change. For instance, early in one's career, receiving a huge pay raise or a promotion might be defined as having achieved success, but later in one's career, experiencing a sense of contentment might be of higher value and also be considered a marker of success.

It is also important to note that there are several pathways to success. For John, the pathway to achieving a salary bump, and later a promotion, was through forging a high-quality relationship with his boss, Peter. Of course, it was not just having a high-quality relationship that resulted in John's success. He also excelled in his position and contributed to the organization. Nevertheless, developing a high-quality relationship was instrumental to his success and was his pathway, so to speak.

"Jill too had a successful career at her previous workplace. When she became vice president of HR, she studied the HR function and concluded two of her four areas needed improvement. She carefully considered whether to initiate large- or small-scale changes to improve the two areas that were most dysfunctional. She rightly chose to initiate small-scale changes, as those were the ones she had the most control over. Small-scale changes lead to small wins, and small wins not only boosted her self-efficacy—meaning her confidence in her ability to get things done—but also attracted allies, which made it possible for her to achieve a string of successes. Small wins and enhanced self-efficacy beliefs served as pathways for Jill's success.

"Now, let's discuss Chris. He was a contender for the warehouse manager position and was very hopeful of getting the job. When he did not get the job, he felt hopeless about his future within the organization. In addition, his current job had become routine and boring. He was experiencing job content and hierarchical plateaus. Instead of ruminating over his unfortunate circumstances and falling into a downward spiral, Chris decided to turn things around by proactively engaging in job crafting. He decreased hindering job demands by delegating job duties he no longer wished to perform and engaged in *approach crafting* by increasing structural resources in the way of voluntarily taking on a workflow project and upskilling through completing a program on data analytics. He also engaged in *relational crafting* by increasing his social resources—forming close relationships at work and with others he had met while pursuing the data analytics program—and, over time, fell back in love with his work. As a result, Jennifer promoted him to the assistant warehouse manager position, which she'd created at that store location just for him. For Chris, job crafting was the pathway to his success.

"Sarah, through her early childhood experiences, developed the ability to be adaptable, and this translated into career adaptability as she transitioned from college to the workforce. Her career adaptability led her to engage in proactive career behaviors, contributing to her promotion to the role of senior data analyst, obtaining the job of director of information security at a second company, and her recent job as vice president of data and information security at a Fortune 500 company. Career adaptability is arguably the root of Sarah's phenomenal success.

"Shawn learned to be compassionate from his mom, and he developed his political skills through observing his dad interact with his subordinates. He honed these qualities in high school and used them to achieve success in school and later in his sales career. His political skills enabled him to build a favorable reputation among others, which was instrumental in his leadership of sales organizations at two different companies. He was able to leverage his political skills to build social capital at Custom Works India, and when the opportunity presented itself, he was promoted to the role of general manager. Shawn's political skills were the pathway to his success.

"Kim and Kathy were successful in their own ways. Kathy, by adopting a prevention focus, made risk-averse decisions—and for her happiness, this was an indicator of success. Kim, on the other hand, adopted a promotion focus, was risk seeking, and took chances that resulted in progressing in her organization. For Kim, achieving career progression was an indicator of success.

"The inequities Darnell witnessed growing up enabled him to develop a deep sense of fairness and social justice. At work, he witnessed unfairness in the performance appraisal process and how it negatively affected his coworkers. So, when Darnell became a manager, he ensured *distributive justice* by allocating performance ratings based on one's contributions, *procedural justice* by developing fair procedures for evaluating performance and codifying this process, and *interactional justice* by ensuring he treated others in a respectful and courteous manner and by candidly communicating performance feedback and tailoring it to meet his subordinates' needs.

"For Darnell, success as a manager meant ensuring fairness in the performance appraisal process and creating a fair work environment. The pathway to Darnell's success was ensuring fairness, which led his subordinates to enhance their performance, engage in citizenship behaviors, and make constructive suggestions to further improve the work environment.

"Michael quit his job when it proved unbearable. When he joined Providence to head the Tulsa office, the work environment was stressful, especially for therapists. Michael identified factors contributing to the high levels of stress and eliminated hindrance job demands by reducing these demands to a manageable level. He also increased job resources by involving therapists in the selection of their clients, increasing management support, and offering professional development opportunities. Michael was able to reduce stress levels, thus achieving success. Successfully applying the job demands-resources model and using the force field analysis was the pathway to Michael's success.

"From these eight stories, you can see there are several pathways to achieve success. To be sure, there are many others, so this list of pathways is illustrative, not exhaustive. The point is, depending on your situation and your circumstance, you can create your *own* pathway to achieve the success *you* desire and rejuvenate your career, health, and happiness."

▧　▧　▧

J Mo concluded the night by saying, "Thank you all for spending a week with us. This has been one of the most remarkable weeks of my career. It has been a real pleasure getting to know each of you." Everyone thanked J Mo for his insights and for inspiring them go back into the world feeling rejuvenated.

TABLE — SUMMARY OF ACTIONS AND OUTCOMES

Forging a High-Quality Relationship with Your Supervisor

Leaders don't treat all their team members the same way. They often differentiate among team members and develop either high- or low-quality relationships with team members. High-quality relationships are based on mutual obligation and reciprocity, characterized by mutual liking and respect, and are often transformational in nature. Followers in high-quality relationship with leaders receive many benefits including challenging assignments, access to information and resources, higher performance evaluations and more promotional opportunities.

Actions to take

- Find common ground with your supervisor.
- Find opportunities to socialize with your supervisor.
- Excel at your job.
- Maintain a positive attitude.
- Relate well with others.
- Volunteer and show initiative.

- Offer constructive suggestions.
- Make your supervisor look good.

Outcomes you can expect

- A high-quality relationship.
- Increased access to your supervisor.
- More resources.
- Challenging job assignments.
- Higher performance evaluations.
- Higher pay raises.
- More promotion opportunities.

Go Big or Go Home vs. Small Wins and Self-Efficacy

The strategy of small wins involves breaking down a complex problem into smaller problems and pursuing a concrete solution to the smaller problem, and thus achieving a small win. A small win attracts resources and sets you up to successfully attempt a slightly larger win, putting you on the course to solving the complex problem.

Actions to take

- Recast big problems into small(er) problems.
- Find a concrete solution to the problem.

Outcomes to expect

- Solving the problem results in a small win.
- Small wins or changes elicit little resistance, are perceived as within one's capability, and are easily accomplished.

- With every small win, you attract more support and resources positioning you well for the next small win.
- A series of small wins gets you closer to your overall goal.

Turning Mundane Work into Exciting Work – Enhancing Work Engagement through Job Crafting

Job crafting is achieved through increasing structural resources, such as autonomy or pursuing developmental opportunities; increasing social resources, such as social support or developing quality social relationships; increasing challenging job demands, such as taking on additional responsibilities or taking on new projects; and lastly, decreasing hindering job demands, such as tasks that are not motivational but drain resources. Job crafting increases work engagement, a fulfilling, work-related state of mind that is characterized by vigor, dedication, and absorption.

Actions to take

- Classify your job duties into three categories: tasks that fit your strengths, fit your interests, and tasks that you no longer wish to perform.
- To the extent possible, try to delegate tasks you no longer wish to perform.
- Engage in approach crafting by increasing structural resources and challenging job demands.
- Engage in relational crafting by seeking ways to increase your social resources.
- Over time, you will be able to transform your mundane job into one that is intrinsically motivating, and you will experience

vigor, dedication, and absorption, thereby increasing your work engagement.

Outcomes to expect

- Reduced perceptions of hierarchical and job content plateaus.
- Increased work engagement, so your job is intrinsically rewarding, motivating, and meaningful.
- Engaged employees receive higher performance evaluations and are more likely to be promoted.
- Being engaged in your job has many positive health benefits, such as enhanced psychological well-being.

Enhancing Career Success through Career Adaptability and Proactive Behaviors

According to Mark Savickas, career adaptability is a psychosocial construct that denotes an individual's resources for coping with current and anticipated tasks, transitions, and traumas in their occupational roles. Career adaptability is a malleable construct which means individuals can work toward increasing their career adaptability.

Actions to take

- To enhance your career adaptability, be willing to explore, learn, grow, change, and adapt.
- Curiosity – Develop your curiosity and explore different vocational possibilities.
- Concern – Be concerned about your future and take advantage of developmental opportunities.

- Control – Take control by engaging in upskilling.
- Confidence – Be confident by believing in your capabilities.

Outcomes to expect

- Career adaptability will help you thrive in a changing, dynamic environment.
- You will have the ability to successfully navigate transitions.
- You will be positioned to take advantage of opportunities as they come along and create new opportunities.

Enhancing Reputation through Political Skill

How we see ourselves reflects our identity. Reputation is in the eye of the beholder and is reflected in how one is perceived and described by others. Social skill moderates this relationship, such that individuals who are socially skilled will be perceived by others in the same way they see themselves. Political skill is a type of social skill that enables individuals to build a favorable reputation and benefit from consequences that come with having a favorable reputation.

Actions to take

- To become more politically skilled, enhance the following four competencies:
    - Apparent sincerity – Be genuine in your interactions, so people perceive you as someone who is sincere and genuinely cares about them.
    - Social astuteness – Develop social astuteness, which is the ability to read a situation and discern cues about

the appropriate thing to say or do in the given situation and to sense hidden motivations and agendas of others.

- ○ Networking ability – Network to develop social connections, as the more positive relationships you have, the better. The more networked you are, the higher your social capital.

- ○ Interpersonal influence – Increase your interpersonal influence by making people comfortable around you, communicating effectively, establishing a good rapport, and getting people to like you.

Outcomes to expect

- Ability to get along well with others.
- A positive reputation.
- Ability to easily navigate organizational politics.
- Likely to emerge as a leader.
- Receive higher performance evaluations.
- Higher likelihood of being promoted.

Adopting a Promotion Focus to Facilitate Career Outcomes

People vary in how they approach pleasure and avoid pain. Such variance is reflected by the regulatory focus, which distinguishes promotion focus from prevention focus. People who are promotion focused desire to improve their status, are risk seeking, and are motivated by gains. Prevention focused individuals desire to protect what they have, are risk averse, and are motivated to avoid losses. We make decisions all the time. Getting better at making good decisions is key to a successful and happy life.

Actions to take

- Know your preferred orientation (i.e., are you a promotion or a prevention focused individual?).
- To become more promotion focused, focus on potential gains and take risks to achieve a better future.
- To become more prevention focused, focus on potential losses and avoid risks to maintain status-quo.
- When making decisions, evaluate options from both frameworks (i.e., switch from one to the other).

Outcome to expect

- Awareness of how you approach decision-making, whether promotion or prevention focused.
- Ability to switch focus and thoroughly evaluate options.
- Ability to make best possible decisions.

Enhancing Performance through Fairness and Feedback

If you supervise employees, you will be required to evaluate the performance of those employees, provide them with feedback, and allocate pay raises. Ensuring fairness is key to building a performance-oriented culture and enhancing the contribution of your unit.

Actions to take

- Distributive justice – To ensure distributive justice, you should be aware of the contributions of your employees and assign performance ratings that are proportional to their contributions.
- Procedural justice – Ensure the procedures used to evaluate performance are fair, free from bias, and apply them consistently to assign performance ratings.
- Interactional justice – Make sure you provide feedback in a clear and candid manner and tailor your performance feedback to the individual. Also, treat employees with respect, dignity, and common courtesy when providing feedback.
- Your employees should be satisfied with the feedback and perceive the feedback as useful, so they can use the feedback to make changes and improve performance.

Outcomes to expect

- Employees will perceive the performance appraisal process to be fair.
- You will succeed in building a performance-oriented culture.
- Employees' performance will increase.
- Employees will engage in citizenship behaviors toward other employees and toward you.
- Employees' work engagement will increase.

Enhancing Psychological Well-Being by Balancing Job Demands and Resources

Every aspect of work can be classified as a job demand or a job resource. By increasing job resources while simultaneously reducing job demands, you will be able to help employees maintain functional stress levels, enhance their psychological well-being, and benefit the organization through enhanced performance and contributions.

Actions to take

- Use the job demands-resources framework to analyze the work environment.
- Identify job demands facing the employees.
- Classify those demands into challenge and hinderance demands, then reduce hindrance demands.
- Increase job resources – You can increase employees' personal resources (through training and giving them more autonomy), provide more support (supervisor resources), and increase organizational resources (e.g., hire more people, use outside consultant).
- The goal should be to increase resources and reduce demands.

Outcomes to expect

- Lower stress levels of employees, less burnout.
- Enhanced psychological well-being of employees.
- A healthy work environment.
- Employees more likely to offer constructive suggestions.
- Increased employee performance and citizenship behaviors.

EXERCISE 1

(To be performed individually)

Describe your job – What are your key responsibilities and what is expected of you?

Describe the work environment – How would you characterize your relationships with your supervisor, coworkers, and peers?

Describe how you feel about your job and your work environment.

What are your aspirational goals? What would you like to achieve? List two to three goals you want to achieve.

[For your unit: some examples include reduce stress in the workplace, create a fair workplace, improve employee performance, streamline work processes, and improve efficiencies. For yourself: some examples include have a better relationship with your supervisor, become a better performer, get the next promotion, and move up in the organization.]

1. List and clearly describe your goal (aspirational goal 1).

2. Identify pathways discussed in this book that are relevant to your goal. Briefly describe how and why they are relevant.

3. List steps you will engage in to implement the ideas from the pathways you have identified as relevant.

4. Set a timeline for what will be accomplished by when.

5. List resources available to you to help achieve your goal.

6. List resources you will need (more training, better network, etc.) to achieve your goal.

7. Develop a plan to get needed resources (what *you* will do to get them).

8. What obstacles will prevent you from achieving your goal?

9. Develop a plan to overcome those obstacles.

10. Considering resources and obstacles, revisit the actions steps (from step 3) you will engage in to achieve your goal. List them along with a timeline for accomplishing each action.

EXERCISE 2

(To be performed with a partner)

You and your partner will individually respond to the following questions.

Describe your job – What are your key responsibilities and what is expected of you?

Describe the work environment – How would you characterize your relationships with your supervisor, coworkers, and peers?

Describe how you feel about your job and your work environment.

What are your aspirational goals? What would you like to achieve? List two to three goals you want to achieve.

[For your unit: some examples include reduce stress in the workplace, create a fair workplace, improve employee performance, streamline work processes, and improve efficiencies. For yourself: some examples include have better relationship with my supervisor, become a better performer, get the next promotion, and move up in the organization.]

1. List and clearly describe your goal (aspirational goal 1).

2. Identify pathways discussed in this book that are relevant to your goal. Briefly describe how and why they are relevant.

3. List steps you will engage in to implement the ideas from the pathways you have identified as relevant.

4. Set a timeline for what will be accomplished by when.

5. List resources available to you to help achieve your goal.

6. List resources you will need (more training, better network, etc.) to achieve your goal.

7. Develop a plan to get needed resources (what *you* will do to get them).

8. What obstacles will prevent you from achieving your goal?

9. Develop a plan to overcome those obstacles.

10. Considering resources and obstacles, revisit the actions steps (from step 3) you will engage in to achieve your goal. List them along with a timeline for accomplishing each action.

Exchange your work, read your partner's work, and offer constructive feedback.

Listen carefully to the feedback you receive from your partner and revise your plan accordingly.

In the light of the feedback received, revisit the actions steps in your plan to achieve your goal. List them along with a timeline for accomplishing each action.

REFERENCES

Forging High-Quality Relationships: Why Does Your Relationship with Your Supervisor Matter?

Bass, B. M. (1985). Leadership and performance beyond expectations, Free Press New York.

Bauer, T.N., & Green, S.G. (1996). Development of leader-member exchange: A longitudinal test. *Academy of Management Journal*, 39, 1538-1567.

Dienesch, R. M., & Liden, R. C. (1986). Leader-member exchange model of leadership: A critique and further development. *Academy of Management Review*, 11, 618-634.

Dulac, T., Coyle-Shapiro, J. A-M., Henderson, D.J., & Wayne, S. J. (2008). Not all responses to breach are the same: The interconnection of social exchange and psychological contract processes in organizations. *Academy of Management Journal*, 51, 1079-1098.

Dulebohn, J.H., Bommer, W.H., Liden, R.C., Brouer, R.L., & Ferris, G.R. (2012). A meta-analysis of antecedents and consequences of leader-member exchange: Integrating the past with an eye toward the future. *Journal of Management*, 38, 1715-1759.

Erdogan, B., & Bauer, T. N. (2014). Leader-member exchange (LMX) theory: The relational approach to leadership. In D. Day (Ed), The Oxford handbook of leadership and organizations (pp. 407-433), Oxford University Press, Oxford, UK.

Erdogan, B., & Liden, R.C. (2002). Social exchanges in the workplace: A review of recent developments and future research directions in leader-member exchange theory. In L. L. Neider & C. A. Schriesheim (Eds.), Leadership (pp. 65-114).

Gerstner, C.R., & Day, D. V. (1997). Meta-analytic review of leader-member exchange theory: Correlates and construct issues. *Journal of Applied Psychology*, 82, 827-844.

Graen, G.B., & Scandura, T.A. (1987). Toward a theory of dyadic organizing. *Research in Organizational Behavior*, 9, 175-208.

Ilies, R., Nahrgang, J.D., & Morgeson, F.P. (2007). Leader-member exchange and citizenship behaviors: A meta-analysis. *Journal of Applied Psychology*, 92, 269-277.

Jawahar, I.M., Stone, T.H., & Kluemper, D. (2019). When and why leaders trust followers: LMX as a mediator and empowerment as a moderator of the trustworthiness-trust relationship. *Career Development International*, 24 (7), 702-716.

Liden, R.C., & Maslyn, J.M. (1998). Multidimensionality of leader-member exchange: An empirical assessment through scale development. *Journal of Management*, 24, 43-72.

Liden, R.C., Sparrowe, R.T., & Wayne, S.J. (1997). Leader-member exchange theory: The past and potential for the future. *Research in Personnel and Human Resources Management*, 15, 47-119.

Martin, R., Guillaume, Y., Thomas, G., Lee, A., & Epitropaki, O. (2016). Leader-member exchange (LMX) and performance: A meta-analytic review. *Personnel Psychology*, 69, 67-121.

Maslyn, J.M., & Uhl-Bien, M. (2001). Leader-member exchange and its dimensions: Effects of self-effort and other's effort on relationship quality. *Journal of Applied Psychology*, 86 (4), 697-708.

Schermuly, C.C., & Meyer, B. (2016). Good relationships at work: The effects of leader-member exchange and team-member exchange on psychological empowerment, emotional exhaustion, and depression. *Journal of Organizational Behavior*, 37, 673-691.

Schriesheim, C.A., Castro, S.L., & Cogliser, C.C. (1999). Leader-member exchange (LMX) research: A comprehensive review of theory, measurement, and data-analytic practices. *Leadership Quarterly*, 10, 63-113.

Sparrowe, R.T., & Liden, R.C. (2005). Two routes to influence: Integrating leader-member exchange and social network perspectives. *Administrative Science Quarterly*, 50, 505-535.

Van Breukelen, W., Schyns, B., & Le Blanc, P. (2006). Leader-member exchange theory and research: Accomplishments and future challenges. *Leadership*, 2, 295-316.

Go Big or Go Home vs. Small Wins and Self-Efficacy

Amabile, T.M., & Kramer, S.J., (2011). The progress principle: Using small wins to ignite joy, engagement, and creativity at work. Boston, MA: Harvard Business School Press.

Amabile, T.M., Kramer, S.J. (May 2011). The power of small wins. Harvard Business Review. https://store.hbr.org/product/the-power-of-small-wins/r1105c?sku=R1105C-PDF-SPA. Accessed July 13, 2021.

Bandura, A. (1977a). Self-efficacy: Toward a unifying theory of behavioral change. *Psychological Review, 84*, 191-215.

Bandura, A. (1977b). *Social learning theory*. Englewood Cliffs, NJ: Prentice Hall.

Bandura, A. (1986). *Social foundations of thought and action: A social cognitive theory*. Englewood Cliffs, NJ: Prentice Hall.

Bandura, A., & Cervone, D. (1983). Self-evaluative and self-efficacy mechanisms governing the motivational effects of goal systems. *Journal of Personality and Social Psychology*, 45, 1017–1028.

Cornell, S.J. (2017). Reducing gender bias in modern workplaces: A small wins approach to organizational change. *Gender & Society*, 13 (6), 725-750.

Davis, M. S. (1971). That's interesting: Towards a phenomenology of sociology and a sociology of phenomenology. *Philosophy of Social Science, 1,* 309-344.

Dohrenwend, B. S., Krasnoff, L., Askenasy, A. R., & Dohrenwend, B. P. (1978). Exemplification of a method for scaling life events: The PERI life events scale. *Journal of Health and Social Behavior, 19,* 205-229

Freedman, J. L., & Fraser, S. C. (1966). Compliance without pressure: The foot-in-the-door technique. *Journal of Personality and Social Psychology, 4,* 195-202.

Hollander, S. (1965). *The sources of increased efficiency: A study of DuPont rayon plants.* Cambridge, MA: MIT Press.

Holsti, O. R. (1978). Limitations of cognitive abilities in the face of crisis. In C. F. Smart & W. T. Stanbury (Eds.), *Studies on crisis management (pp.* 35-55). Toronto: Butterworth.

Jawahar, I, M. & Mohammed, Z. (in press). Process management self-efficacy: Scale development and validation. *Journal of Business and Psychology.*

Judge, T. A., & Bono, J. E. (2001). Relationship of core self-evaluations trait—self-esteem, generalized self-efficacy, locus of control, and emotional stability—with job satisfaction and job performance: A meta-analysis. *Journal of Applied Psychology, 86,* 80-92.

Kohn, M. L. (1976). Looking back—A 25-year review and appraisal of social problems research. *Social Problems, 24,* 94-112.

Rigotti, T., Schyns, B., & Mohr, G. (2008). A short version of the occupational self-efficacy scale: Structural and construct validity across five countries. *Journal of Career Assessment,* 16 (2), 238-255.

Sarason, S. B. (1978). The nature of problem solving in social action. *American Psychologist, 33,* 370-380.

Stajkovic, A. D., & Luthans, F. (1998). Self-efficacy and work-related performance: A meta-analysis. *Psychological Bulletin, 124,* 240-261.

Weick, K. E. (1984). Small wins: Redefining the scale of social problems. *American Psychologist,* 39 (1), 40-49.

Turning Mundane Work into Exciting Work: Enhancing Work Engagement through Job Crafting

Allen, T. D., Russell, J. E., Poteet, M. L., & Dobbins, G. H. (1999). Learning and development factors related to perceptions of job content and hierarchical plateauing. *Journal of Organizational Behavior,* 20, 1113–1137.

Bakker, A. B. (2010). Engagement and "job crafting": Engaged employees create their own great place to work. In S. L. Albrecht (Ed.), *Handbook of employee engagement: Perspectives, issues, research and practice* (pp. 229–244). Northampton, MA: Edward Elgar Publishing.

Bakker, A. B. (2011). An evidence-based model of work engagement. *Current Directions in Psychological Science, 20,* 265–269.

Bakker, A. B., & Albrecht, S. (2018). Work engagement: Current trends. *Career Development International, 23,* 4–11.

Bakker, A. B., Tims, M., & Derks, D. (2012). Proactive personality and job performance: The role of job crafting and work engagement. *Human Relations, 65*(10), 1359–1378.

Bardwick, J. M. (1986). The plateauing trap. New York, NY: AMACOM

Berg, J. M., Dutton, J. E., & Wrzesniewski, A. (2013). Job crafting and meaningful work. In B. J. Dik, Z. S. Byrne, & M. F. Steger (Eds.), *Purpose and meaning in the workplace* (pp. 81–104). Washington, DC: American Psychological Association

Bipp, T., & Demerouti, E. (2015). Which employees craft their jobs and how? Basic dimensions of personality and employees' job crafting behaviour. *Journal of Occupational and Organizational Psychology*, *88*(4), 631–655.

Bruning, P. F., & Campion, M. A. (2018). A role–resource approach-avoidance model of job crafting: A multimethod integration and extension of job crafting theory. *Academy of Management Journal*, *61*(2), 499–522.

Demerouti, E., Bakker, A. B., Nachreiner, F., & Schaufeli, W. B. (2001). The job demands-resources model of burnout. *Journal of Applied psychology*, *86*(3), 499–512.

Hofstetter, H., & Cohen, A. (2014). The mediating role of job content plateau on the relationship between work experience characteristics and early retirement and turnover intentions. Personnel Review, 43, 350–376.

Kuijpers, E., Kooij, D., van Woerkom, M. (2020). Align your job with yourself: The relationship between a job crafting intervention and work engagement, and the role of workload. *Journal of Occupational Health Psychology*, 25 (1), 1-16.

Lapalme, M., Tremblay, M., & Simard, G. (2009). The relationship between career plateauing, employee commitment and psychological distress: The role of organizational and supervisor support. *International Journal of Human Resource Management*, 20, 1132–1145.

Lazazzara, A., Tims, M., & de Gennaro, D. (2020). The process of re-inventing a job: A meta-synthesis of qualitative job crafting research. *Journal of Vocational Behavior.*

Shabeer, S., Mohammed, S.J., Jawahar, I.M., & Bilal, A.R. (2019). The mediating influence of fit-perceptions in the relationship between career adaptability and job content and hierarchical plateaus. *Journal of Career Development*, 46 (3), 332-345.

Tims, M., & Bakker, A. B. (2010). Job crafting: Towards a new model of individual job redesign. *SA Journal of Industrial Psychology, 36*(2), 1–9.

Tims, M., Bakker, A. B., & Derks, D. (2012). Development and validation of the job crafting scale. *Journal of Vocational Behavior, 80*(1), 173–186.

Tims, M., Derks, D., & Bakker, A. B. (2016). Job crafting and its relationships with person–job fit and meaningfulness: A three-wave study. *Journal of Vocational Behavior, 92*, 44–53.

Wrzesniewski, A., & Dutton, J. E. (2001). Crafting a job: Revisioning employees as active crafters of their work. *The Academy of Management Review, 26*(2), 179–201.

Wrzesniewski, A., LoBuglio, N., Dutton, J. E., & Berg, J. M. (2013). Job crafting and cultivating positive meaning and identity in work.

Advances in positive organizational psychology (pp. 281–302). Emerald Group Publishing Limited.

Zhang, F., & Parker, S. K. (2018). Reorienting job crafting research: A hierarchical structure of job crafting concepts and integrative review. *Journal of Organizational Behavior.*

Zhang, F., Wang, B., Qian, J., & Parker, S.K. (2021). Job crafting towards strengths and job crafting towards interests in overqualified employees: Different outcomes and boundary effects. *Journal of Organizational Behavior.*

Enhancing Career Success through Career Adaptability and Proactive Behaviors

Bimrose, J., & Hearne, L. (2012). Resilience and career adaptability: Qualitative studies of adult career counseling. Journal of Vocational Behavior, 81, 338–344. doi:10.1016/j.jvb.2012.08.002

Douglass, R. P., & Duffy, R. D. (2014). Calling and career adaptability among undergraduate students. Journal of Vocational Behavior, 86, 58–65. doi:10.1016/j.jvb.2014.11.003

Fiori, M., Bollmann, G., & Rossier, J. (2015). Exploring the path through which career adaptability increases job satisfaction and lowers job stress: The role of affect. Journal of Vocational Behavior. Advance online version. doi:10.1016/j.jvb.2015.08.010

Haenggli, M. & Hirschi, A. (2020). Career adaptability and career success in the context of broader career resources framework. Journal of Vocational Behavior, 119, https://doi.org/10.1016/j.jvb.2020.103414

Johnston, C. S. (2016). A systematic review of the career adaptability literature and future outlook. Journal of Career Assessment, 26, 1–28. https://doi.org/10.1177/1069072716679921

Rudolph, C.W., Lavigne, K.N., Katz, I.M., & Zacher, H. (2017). Linking dimensions of career adaptability to adaptation results: A meta-analysis. Journal of Vocational Behavior, 102, 151-173.

Savickas, M. L. (1997). Career adaptability: An integrative construct for life-span, life-space theory. The Career Development Quarterly, 45(3), 247–259.

Savickas, M. L. (2005). The theory and practice of career construction. Career development and counseling: Putting theory and research to work. Vol. 1. Career development and counseling: Putting theory and research to work (pp. 42–70).

Savickas, M. L. (2013). Career construction theory and practice. In S. D. B. R. W. L. (Ed.). Career development and counseling: Putting theory and research to work (pp. 42–70). (2nd ed.). Hoboken, NJ: Wiley.

Savickas, M. L., & Porfeli, E. J. (2012). Career adapt-abilities scale: Construction, reliability, and measurement equivalence across 13 countries. Journal of Vocational Behavior, 80(3), 661–673.

Spurk, D., Volmer, J., Orth, M., & Goritz, A.S. (2020). How career adaptability and proactive career behaviors interrelate over time? An inter- and intraindividual investigation. Journal of Occupational and Organizational Psychology, 29, 158-186.

Negru-Subtirica, O., Pop, E. I., & Crocetti, E. (2015). Developmental trajectories and reciprocal associations between career adaptability and vocational identity: A three-wave longitudinal study with adolescents. Journal of Vocational Behavior, 88, 131–142. https://doi.org/10.1016/j.jvb.2015.03.004

Zacher, H. (2014a). Career adaptability predicts subjective career success above and beyond personality traits and core self-evaluations. Journal of Vocational Behavior, 84, 21–30. doi:10.1016/j.jvb.2013.10.002

*Zacher, H. (2014b). Individual difference predictors of change in career adaptability over time. Journal of Vocational Behavior, 84, 188–198. doi:10.1016/j.jvb.2014.01.001

Zacher, H. (2015). Daily manifestations of career adaptability: Relationships with job and career outcomes. Journal of Vocational Behavior, 91, 76–86. https://doi.org/10.1016/j.jvb.2015.09.003

Enhancing Reputation through Political Skill

Blickle, G., Frohlich, J., Ehlert, S., Pirner, K., Dietl, E., Hanes, T., & Ferris, G. R. (2011). Socio-analytic theory and work behavior: Roles of work values and political skill in job performance and promotability assessment. Journal of Vocational Behavior, 78, 136-148.

Foster, J., Stone, T.H., Jawahar, I.M., & Brigitte, S. (2021). Reputational self-awareness: Predicting how others view your personality. *International Journal of Selection and Assessment.*

Ferris, G. R., Blickle, G., Schneider, P., Kramer, J., Zettler, I., Solga, J., Noethen, D., & Meurs, J. (2008). Political skill construct and criterion-related validation: A two-study investigation. *Journal of Managerial Psychology*, 23, 744-771.

Ferris, G. R., Treadway, D., Brouer, R., & Munyon, T. (2012). Political skill in the organizational sciences. In G. Ferris & D. Treadway (Eds.), *Politics in organizations: Theory and research considerations*: 487-529. New York: Routledge/Taylor and Francis.

Ferris, G. R., Treadway, D., Kolodinsky, R., Hochwarter, W., Kacmar, C., Douglas, C., & Frink, D. (2005). Development and validation of the *Political Skill Inventory. Journal of Management*, 31, 126-152.

Ferris, G. R., Treadway, D., Perrewe, P., Brouer, R., Douglas, C., & Lux, S. (2007). Political skill in organizations. *Journal of Management*, 33, 290-320.

Hogan, R. (1983). A socio-analytic theory of personality. In M. M. Page (Ed.), *1982 Nebraska symposium on motivation* (pp. 55–89). Lincoln, NE: University of Nebraska Press.

Hogan, J. & Holland, B. (2003). Using theory to evaluate personality and job-performance relations: A socio-analytic perspective. *Journal of Applied Psychology, 88*, 100–112.

Hogan, R. & Blickle, G. (2018). Socio-analytic theory: Basic concepts, supporting evidence and practical implications. In V. Zeigler-Hill & T. K. Shackelford (Eds.), *The SAGE handbook of personality and individual differences: The science of personality and individual differences* (p. 110–129).

Johnson, D.E., Erez, A., Kiker, D.S. and Motowildo, S.J. (2002). Liking and attributions of motives as mediators of the relationships between individuals' reputations: helpful behaviors, and raters' reward decisions. *Journal of Applied Psychology*, 87, 808-815.

Laird, M.D., Zboja, J.J., Martinez, A.D., & Ferris, G.R. (2013). Performance and political skill in personal reputation assessments. *Journal of Managerial Psychology*, 28 (6), 661-676.

Munyon, T. P., Summers, J. K., Thompson, K. W., & Ferris, G. R. (2015). Political skill and work outcomes: A theoretical extension, meta-analytic investigation, and agenda for the future. *Personnel Psychology*, 68, 143-184.

Wihler, A., Blickle, G., Ellen III, B.P., Hochwarter, A.A., & Ferris, G.R. (2017). Personal initiative and job performance evaluations: Role of political skill in opportunity recognition and capitalization. *Journal of Management*, 43 (5), 1388-1420.

Adopting a Promotion Focus to Facilitate Career Outcomes

Crowe, E., & Higgins, E. T. (1997). Regulatory focus and strategic inclinations: Promotion and prevention in decision-making. *Organizational Behavior and Human Decision Processes*, 69, 117–132

Higgins, E. T. (1997). Beyond pleasure and pain. American Psychologist, 52, 1280–1300.

Higgins, E.T. (1987). Self-discrepancy: A theory relating self and affect. *Psychological Review*, 94(3), 319–340.

Higgins, E.T. (1998a). From expectancies to worldviews: Regulatory focus in socialization and cognition. In J.M. Darley & J. Cooper (Eds.), *Attribution and social interaction: The legacy of Edward E. Jones* (pp. 243–269). Washington, DC: American Psychological Association.

Higgins, E.T. (1998b). Promotion and prevention: Regulatory focus as a motivational principle. *Advances in Experimental Social Psychology*, 30, 1–46.

Higgins, E.T. (2000a). Making a good decision: Value from fit. *American Psychologist*, 55(11), 1217–1230.

Higgins, E.T. (2000b). Social cognition: Learning about what matters in the social world. *European Journal of Social Psychology*, 30, 3–39.

Molden, D. C., Lee, A. Y., & Higgins, E. T. (2008). Motivation for promotion and prevention. In J. Shah & W. Gardner (Eds.), *Handbook of motivation science* (pp. 169–187). New York, NY: Guilford Press.

Molden, D. C., & Higgins, E. T. (2005). Motivated thinking. In K. J. Holyoak & R. G. Morrison (Eds.), *The Cambridge handbook of thinking and reasoning* (pp. 295–317). New York, NY: Cambridge University Press.

Scholer, A. A., Ozaki, Y., & Higgins, E. T. (2014). Inflating and deflating the self: Sustaining motivation concerns through self-evaluation. *Journal of Experimental Social Psychology, 51,* 60–73.

Shin, Y., Kim, M.S., Choi, J.N., Kim, M. and Oh, W.-K. (2017). Does leader-follower regulatory fit matter? The role of regulatory fit in followers' organizational citizenship behavior. *Journal of Management,* 43 (4), 1211-1233.

Spanjol, J., & Tam, L. (2010). To change or not to change: how regulatory focus affects change in dyadic decision-making creativity and innovation management regulatory focus and change in dyadic decision-making. *Creativity & Innovation Management,* 19 (4), 346-363.

Tu, Y., Long., L., Wang, H., & Jiang, L. (2019). To prevent or to promote: How regulatory focus moderates the differentiated effects of quantitative versus qualitative job insecurity on employee stress and motivation. *International Journal of Stress Management,* 27 (2), 134-145.

Enhancing Performance through Fairness and Feedback

Adams, S. (1965). Inequity in Social Exchange. In Leonard Berkowitz, ed. *Advances in Experimental Social Psychology* (pp. 267-299). New York: Academic Press.

Bies, R.J. (2001). Interactional in (justice): The sacred and the profane. In Greenberg, J. and Cropanzano, R. (Eds.), *Advances in Organizational Justice* (pp. 89-118). Stanford University Press: Stanford, CA.

Bies, R., & Moag, J.S (1986). Interactional justice: Communication criteria of fairness", in Lewicki, R.J., Sheppard, B.H. and Bazerman, M. (Eds.), *Research on Negotiation in Organization* 99. 43-55). JAI Press: Greenwich, CT.

Colquitt, J. A. (2001). On the dimensionality of organizational justice: A construct validation of a measure. *Journal of Applied Psychology*, 86, 386-400.

Colquitt, J.A., Conlon, D.E., Wesson, M.J., Porter, C., & Ng, K.Y. (2001). Justice at the millennium: A meta-analytic review of 25 years of organizational justice research. *Journal of Applied Psychology*, 86, 425-445.

Greenberg, J. (1986). Determinants of perceived fairness of performance evaluations. *Journal of Applied Psychology*, 71, 340-342.

Greenberg, J. (1988). Equity and workplace status: A field experiment. *Journal of Applied Psychology*, 73, 606-613.

Greenberg, J. (1993). The social side of fairness: Interpersonal and informational classes of organizational justice. In Cropanzano, R. (Ed.), *Justice in the workplace: Approaching fairness in human resource management* (pp. 79-103). Erlbaum: Hillsdale, NJ.

Jawahar, I.M. (2007). The influence of perceptions of fairness on performance appraisal reactions. *Journal of Labor Research*, 28, 735-754.

Jawahar, I.M. (2010). The mediating role of appraisal feedback reactions on the relationship between rater feedback-related behaviors and ratee performance. Group & Organization Management, 35 (4), 494-526.

Kluger, A. N., & DeNisi, A. (1996). The effects of feedback interventions on performance: A historical review, meta-analysis and a preliminary feedback intervention theory. Psychological Bulletin, 119, 254-284.

Levy, P. E., & Williams, J. R. (2004). The social context of performance appraisal: A review and framework for the future. Journal of Management, 30, 881-905.

Murphy, K. R., & Cleveland, J. N. (1995). Understanding performance appraisal: Social, organizational and goal-based perspectives. Thousand Oaks, CA: Sage.

Thibaut, J., & Walker, L. (1975), *Procedural Justice: A Psychological Analysis*, Erlbaum, Hillsdale, NJ.

Enhancing Psychological Well-Being by Balancing Job Demands and Resources

Bakker, A. B. (2011). An evidence-based model of work engagement. *Current Directions in Psychological Science, 20,* 265–269.

Bakker, A.B., & Demerouti, E. (2017). Job demands-resources theory: Taking stock and looking forward. *Journal of Occupational Health Psychology,* 22 (3), 273-285.

Bakker, A. B., & Demerouti, E. (2007). The job demands–resources model: State of the art. *Journal of Managerial Psychology, 22,* 309–328.

Bakker, A. B., & Sanz-Vergel, A. I. (2013). Weekly work engagement and flourishing: The role of hindrance and challenge demands. *Journal of Vocational Behavior, 83,* 397–409.

Bakker, A. B., Van Veldhoven, M. J. P. M., & Xanthopoulou, D. (2010). Beyond the Demand-Control model: Thriving on high job demands and resources. *Journal of Personnel Psychology, 9*, 3–16.

Bakker, A. B., Van Emmerik, H., & Van Riet, P. (2008). How job demands, resources, and burnout predict objective performance: A constructive replication. *Anxiety, Stress, and Coping, 21*, 309–324.

Cavanaugh, M. A., Boswell, W. R., Roehling, M. V., & Boudreau, J. W. (2000). An empirical examination of self-reported work stress among US managers. *Journal of Applied Psychology, 85*, 65–74.

Demerouti, E., Bakker, A. B., Nachreiner, F., & Schaufeli, W. B. (2001). The job demands-resources model of burnout. *Journal of Applied Psychology, 86*, 499–512.

Horan, K.A., Nakahara, W.H., DiStaso, M.J., & Jex, S.M. (2020). A review of the challenge-hindrance stress model: Recent advances, expanded paradigms, and recommendations for future research. *Frontiers in Psychology*, 11,

LePine, J. A., Podsakoff, N. P., & LePine, M. A. (2005). A meta-analytic test of the challenge stressor-hindrance stressor framework: An explanation for inconsistent relationships among stressors and performance. *Academy of Management Journal, 48*, 764–775.

McCauley, C. D., Ruderman, M. N., Ohlott, P. J., & Morrow, J. E. (1994). Assessing the developmental components of managerial jobs. *Journal of Applied Psychology, 79*, 544–560.

Searle, B. J., & Auton, J. C. (2015). The merits of measuring challenge and hindrance appraisals. *Anxiety, Stress, and Coping, 28,* 121–143.

Taris, T. W. (2006). Is there a relationship between burnout and objective performance? A critical review of 16 studies. *Work & Stress, 20,* 316–334.

Ten Brummelhuis, L. L., Ter Hoeven, C. L., Bakker, A. B., & Peper, B. (2011). Breaking through the loss cycle of burnout: The role of motivation. *Journal of Occupational and Organizational Psychology, 84,* 268–287.

www.ingramcontent.com/pod-product-compliance
Lightning Source LLC
Chambersburg PA
CBHW071606210326
41597CB00019B/3426